BUSINESS VALUATION MANUAL

An Understandable, Step-By-Step Guide
To Finding The Value Of A Business

Thomas W. Horn

THE BUSINESS VALUATION MANUAL
   An Understandable, Step-By-Step Guide To
   Finding The Value Of A Business

All rights reserved.
Copyright 1985 by Thomas W. Horn ©
This book may not be reproduced or transmitted, in whole or in part, by any means, mechanical or electronic, including photocopying, recording, or information storage and retrieval systems, without express written permission from the author. The tree logo, leaf logo, and name "Charter Oak Press" are the trademarks of the publisher.

Library of Congress Cataloging in Publication Data
Horn, Thomas W.
   THE BUSINESS VALUATION MANUAL
   An Understandable, Step-By-Step Guide To
   Finding The Value Of A Business
   Includes Index
   1. Business Enterprises--Valuation 2. Corporations--Valuation 3. Corporations--Merger 4. Corporations--Finance I. Title.
HD1393.25.H66 1985   658.1'522   85-11636
ISBN 0-87521-015-5

First Printing 1985
Published by

Charter Oak Press
Post Office Box 7783
Lancaster PA 17604

Printed in the United States of America

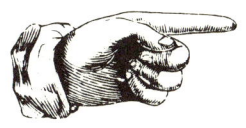 **INTRODUCTORY NOTE**

This book is not meant to be "read" cover to cover. It is a tool which is designed to get you results right away.

Start with Chapter 1. This will tell you how to use the manual and it will provide any preliminary information you may need to know about the basic procedure. Then go on to Chapters 2 and 3. They will instruct you on exactly how to gather and prepare the information you will need in order to do the valuation. Chapter 4 will then tell you exactly which of the valuation methods (contained in Chapters 5 through 13) to use. Of those, you will use only the chapters you need. Finally, wrap up your appraisal by referring to Chapters 14 and 15.

If you are confused by certain terms or concepts, refer to the Glossary contained in the rear of the book for an explanation. Most of the accounting and financial terms used in this manual are defined there. The concepts are defined only within the context of valuation. These terms may have different meanings when used with reference to other topics. An asterisk (*) following a word or phrase means it is defined in the glossary.

You may find the text repetitive if read through completely. But concepts are repeated in each chapter in which they are important so that the user does not have to read every chapter in order to avoid missing something. Occasionally you will be referred back to a step in another chapter, if that idea is important to the method you are using. But it is not necessary to read through any more of that chapter than the part you are referred to.

ACKNOWLEDGMENTS

Special thanks to Clinton Kemp, Esquire; Kathleen Tyler; Mike Wolfe, CPA; Jay Siegrist, CPA; Mel Kohudik; Dan Poynter; Pete Hicks; Woody Peters; and Scott Scheffey.

Introductory Note   3

GETTING STARTED

1- How To Use This Handbook   11

   -You Don't Have to Be a Financial Genius to Use This Handbook   11
   -Rule #1: No Single Figure Will Be Absolutely Correct   12
   -Valuation Methods Always "Assume" The Sale of the Business   14
   -How To Use This Manual: The Basic Procedure   15
   -Why You Should Do A Valuation   16
   -Using Your Valuation As A Negotiating Tool   17
   -Using the Valuation To Predict Whether An Acquisition Is "Doable"   20
   -Using The Valuation To Help Borrow Money   20
   -Valuation Brings You Down To Earth On Price   21

	-Inviting Offers For The Company Just To Try To Find Out What It Is Worth	23
2-	**Getting Ready**	25
	-Learn As Much As You Reasonably Can About The Company	25
	-An Information Checklist To Use	28
	-Talking To Managers and Owners For Further Information	34
3-	**First: "Adjust" The Financial Statements**	37
	-Why Financial Statements Are Adjusted	37
	-What To Adjust And How To Adjust It	39
	-Note on Adjusting Interest Expense	45
	-Note on Partnerships & Sole Proprietorships	46
4-	**Which Methods To Use In Your Case**	49

THE METHODS

5-	**The "Ability To Pay" Method**	55
	-When To Use This Method	55
	-Limitation To This Method	56
	-Brief Description Of The Method	57
	-Steps	58
	-Summary	66
6-	**Discounted Cash Flow Method**	67
	-When To Use This Method	67
	-Brief Description Of The Method	68
	-Steps	69
	-Summary	89
7-	**Capitalization Of Income Stream Method**	91
	-When To Use This Method	92
	-Brief Description Of The Method	92
	-Steps	93
	-Summary	97

8-	**Excess Earnings Method**	99
	-When To Use This Method	99
	-Brief Description Of The Method	99
	-Steps	99
	-Asset Appraisals	100
	-Summary	107
	-Alternative Approach	108
9-	**Economic Value Of Assets Method**	109
	-When To Use This Method	109
	-Which "Measure" Of Value To Use (Market Value vs. Liquidation Value)	110
	-Liquidation Value	112
	-Market Value	113
	-Valuing Intangible Assets - An Overview	115
	*-Note On The Realistic Life Of An Intangible Asset	116
	-Methods Used To Value Intangible Assets:	
	1-Pricing Advantage (or Profit Contribution)	116
	2-Royalty or Licensing Agreements	118
	3-Profit Contribution By Cost Savings	119
	4-Cost To Create The Intangible Asset	120
	5-Cost To Purchase The Intangible Asset	121
	6-Contracts Which Provide Income (Sales Contracts)	121
	7-Employment Contracts	121
10-	**Net Worth Per Books Approach**	123
	-The Concept of "Net Worth" and Its Role In Valuation	123
	-The Definition Of Net Worth (or Book Value) For Valuation Purposes	124
	-When To Use The Net Worth or "Book Value" Approach	124
	-Why Net Worth Is Not A Reliable Measure Of Value	126

11- The Internal Revenue Service Method	127
-When To Use This Method	127
-Brief Description Of The Method	128
-Steps (Summarized)	129
-Special Considerations In Estate Tax Valuations	130
-The Actual Internal Revenue Service Rules (Reproduced)	131
12- Popular Methods You Should Avoid	149
-Comparable Sales Method	150
-Price/Earnings Ratio Method ("Multiple" Of Earnings Method)	153
-Replacement Cost Method	155
-Rule Of Thumb Methods Used For Particular Types Of Businesses ("Industry Method")	156
13- Secured Loan Value	157
-An Explanation of "Secured Loan Value"	157
-How To Determine It	159
-Using Accounts Receivable As Loan Security (Collateral)	160
-Using Inventory As Loan Security	160
-Using Machinery and Equipment As Security	161
-Using Real Estate As Security	162
-Important Limit on Secured Loan Value	164

WRAPPING UP THE VALUATION

14- Some Final Points To Consider In Completing The Valuation	165
-Try To Be Objective and Realistic	166
-Negotiation Will Affect Final Price	166
-Value The Company As It Stands Now	167
-Divorce Situations	168
-When The Bulk Of The Company's Assets Is Inventory	168
-Get An Accountant To Check Over Your Work Before You Rely Upon It	169

-Deduct Any Liabilities Which A Business Buyer Would Assume	169
-Can The Business Pay For Itself At The Assumed Price?	170
-When The Buyer Pays With It's Own Stock	170
-Squaring The Results From The Different Methods ("Correlation of Results")	171
-Other Factors in a Transaction Which Will Affect the Purchase Price	173
15- Will The Business Be Able To Pay For Itself? (Cash Flow Analysis)	183

SOME ADDITIONAL HELPERS

16- Glossary	187
17- Appendix: Present Value Tables	219
18- Index	221

DISCLAIMER

This book is not intended to be a substitute for legal, accounting, or other professional advice, and in providing the information contained herein the author and publisher do not purport to render the same. The use of any part of this book is expressly conditioned upon the user's acknowledgement of his responsibility for seeking competent professional advice for verification of all information contained herein, as well as with regard to its application to any specific circumstances, and prior to making any decision of any type in reliance upon the same or the use thereof or results obtained thereby.

While every effort has been made to make this manual as complete and as accurate as possible within its intended scope, it is not the purpose of this book to present all relevant information available on the topic or all that is necessarily required to conduct a valuation, but rather to compliment, amplify, and supplement other materials and advice available on the subject. The author and the publisher make no representations whatsoever with regard to the reliability of the information contained herein. There may be mistakes contained in the information presented, both typographical and in content, and certain parts may be or become out of date, particularly due to changes in the tax laws. In addition, this material has limited applicability to the valuation publicly-held companies, or interests therein. Qualified investment bankers should be consulted with regard to the latter. These caveats and disclaimers supercede any other representations contained herein or in any other materials.

The author and the publisher shall have no responsibility or liability to any person or entity with respect to any loss, damage, or claim allegedly caused by, related to, or arising out of, either directly or indirectly, the information contained herein or the use thereof.

CHAPTER 1

HOW TO USE THIS HANDBOOK

You Don't Have To Be A Financial Genius To Use This Handbook

This manual is designed to enable virtually anyone to reliably and confidently determine the worth of a business. It is an expanded version of a handbook which was originally written by a mergers and acquisitions professional for his own use in order to make valuation understandable and easy to perform on a regular basis. As a non-accountant, he found that other materials available on the subject seemed too vague or confusing to be consistently helpful. At the same time he wanted to achieve better results than those being offered by the many firms which charge such incredibly high fees to conduct such an appraisal.

This is a ready-to-use guide to valuation - not a technical treatise. The traditional and accepted valuation methods have been broken down into easy to follow steps and spelled out in plain english, so that even someone with no great financial or accounting knowledge can use these respected techniques to reliably determine the value of a business. At the same time, accountants and finance people should find this the most usable guide available on the subject.

The methods have been explained in unusual detail, and there should be no need for background reading. At the same time, however, we have tried to avoid burdening the text with lengthy explanations of terms and concepts. Most of these may already be understood by the user anyway. Therefore, any concepts which may require explanation for some readers have been marked by an asterisk (*) and defined in the Glossary (Chapter 16).

Rule Number One: No Single Figure Will Be Absolutely Correct

This manual guides you carefully through each of the generally accepted methods used by experts. It does not attempt to cover every subtle nuance of valuation that has ever been discovered. This is because valuation is such an inexact science that such subtle refinements are often viewed as a waste of time. For reasons which you will understand better as you get into this, there is no "correct" price or value for any company which governs all circumstances. The number you arrive at through valuation amounts to an educated guess at best. The importance of down-to-the-dollar accuracy can easily get out of hand, and introducing additional complexities to the process generally will not change the results enough to justify the added effort and confusion involved. In most cases, it is simply not a good expense of your time to be so thoroughly exhaustive. Hopefully, this book will guide you past much of the nitpicking and get you good professional results.

Another reason to avoid overdoing it is because, if the value or price of the company is going to be the subject of negotiation, then the figure finally agreed upon by the parties is going to be different from the one you start out with anyway - perhaps substantially so. So don't kill yourself worrying about absolute precision in your results. It is still only going to be a starting point for negotiation.

Since an exact value for a business is such an elusive thing, the fine points that some appraisers might get hung up on can be ignored in most cases. Use your best judgment. However, if you are actually going to make a business or investment decision of any type based upon your results, it is essential to have a qualified accountant review your work. This is to check for errors in your calculations, to verify your methods and assumptions, and to give you a second opinion on matters calling for the exercise of personal judgment. And, if something important has been neglected, you want to make sure that it is brought to your attention. Without an up-to-date knowledge of tax and accounting, it is easy to overlook such things.

You should see by now that valuation is a fairly subjective process. As you go through each method, you will find that there are many occasions when you are called upon to exercise your own personal judgment. This is also apparent at the end of the process, when you compare the results obtained from each method used and decide how much weight to give each one. Two professionals, each using the same procedures and the same raw data, are going to come up with different results at the end. There is nothing wrong with this - it is expected. The only assumption here is that you will be honest and intelligent in exercis-

ing your judgment. Use reliable raw data, be scrupulously truthful, document your results so others can see how you got to them - and then make your decisions confidently. There is room for reasonable variation in results, but make sure that it is indeed "reasonable". As a valuator, one of your goals is to lessen the subjective character of your work, and make the results you obtain as objective as possible.

Valuation Methods Always "Assume" The Sale Of The Business

Most of the methods presented in this book assume that a sale of the business will take place. This is valid even if the study is being undertaken for other purposes, such as estate planning. This is because, with few exceptions, the standard and accepted basis for value, no matter what the figure is used for, is "market value". Market value is that price at which the business is most likely to change hands in an arm's length transaction between buyer and seller, neither being under any particular compulsion to act. The only notable exception to this rule is in the case of appraisals conducted for insurance purposes where the coverage is for the "replacement value" of the assets (a topic treated in Chapter 12). So do not be concerned by the constant references in the text to "buyer", "seller", "acquisition", "purchase", or "sale", even if you are using your valuation for other reasons.

How To Use This Manual: The Basic Procedure

 1- Gather the raw data and information needed for the study. (See Chapter 2)

 2- Consult Chapter 4 to determine which methods to use in your particular case.

 3- Use each applicable method according to its instructions.

 4- Refer to Chapter 14 for instructions on how to wrap up the valuation and correlate* the different results obtained by each method.

 5- If your case involves an acquisition which must pay for itself out of company's cash flow, refer to Chapter 15.

 6- Consult the Glossary (Chapter 16) for an explanation of terms or concepts which you do not understand.

Each time you do a valuation, you will see that there are several methods you can use. Chapter 4 tells you which ones to use in any particular case. One or more may seem right on target. On the other hand, it may appear that no method is exactly made to order for the situation you are dealing with. That is a fairly common situation. However, go through the process using every method which seems the least bit appropriate. Each one will yield a different number, and in the end you will have a <u>range</u> of possible values. You will then compare the results, and assign more weight to those obtained from the methods that seem to fit better. This will tell you <u>where</u> within the range of figures the value of the company is most likely to lie. This process is known as "correlating the results", and it is explained further in Chapter 14. If one method seems to fit the situation like a glove, you can rely on it principally.

Chapter 3 deals with making adjustments to the company's income statements. Where it is necessary to consult that chapter, you will be referred back to it by the instructions for the particular method you are dealing with.

<u>Why You Should Do A Valuation</u>

Most valuations using the methods outlined in this book are conducted for one of the following reasons:
- To prepare for the sale or purchase of a business.
- To prepare for the purchase of a part owner's or stockholder's share in a company.[1]
 (To establish the "buy-sell" value between owners in the event one of them wants to sell, or to at least determine in advance the price formula which will be used, in order to help avoid later disagreements.)
- For the estate planning purposes of the owners, and to avoid overpaying gift and estate taxes by having a well-documented valuation study (to prevent over-appraisal by the IRS).

---

[1]Note: These methods are designed primarily for use with privately-held companies. They also apply well to publicly listed companies whose stock is so closely held (owned by a very small number of parties, and rarely sold or traded) that the company could be considered privately held, despite public registration of its stock.

- Where owners would simply like to measure their success by using company worth as a gauge.
- Where investors in a company want to measure their capital gains or losses to date.
- Where lenders or investors want to verify whether the deal is what it appears to be before they lend or invest (because true economic worth of the company is not reflected in the balance sheet).
- To determine the adequacy of key person life insurance.
- To prepare for corporate or partnership dissolutions.
- To prepare for a reorganization.

Of these uses, the most common will be for the sale or purchase of a business, generally a privately-held one. The remainder of this chapter discusses the use of the valuation study for that purpose.

Using Your Valuation As A Negotiating Tool

A well prepared valuation is generally your best ammunition for negotiating a fair sale price for a business. Any time you walk into a negotiating session you can expect that the other party has done some form of valuation as well, and that his work has yielded a number which is different from yours. That party is going to argue for the use of a method which gives a result most favorable to its own cause. You have got to be prepared to show why that method may be inappropriate in this case, or how it is being improperly implemented.

Right at the bargaining table, you will often find yourselves debating the merits of the valuation methods which might be used in setting the price. You must be prepared, and the only way to know what you are talking about is to have gone through the valuation procedures yourself. If you have not done this, it is going to be very difficult to negotiate effectively on your own behalf. Psychologically, it is also essential to have good, confident feeling for how much value you are buying or selling. Otherwise, you can find yourself "psyched out" by the other party.

This brings up another point. Because this process occurs at the negotiating table, the person who has actually gone through the methods and worked with the figures is probably the only one who understands the results well enough to effectively present your case. If you are going to be the negotiator, then you should do the valuation.

The price that is actually negotiated in any deal is always a compromise between what the seller wants (sometimes a highly subjective figure) and what the company is actually worth to the buyer. It is legitimate to say that the same company can be worth different amounts in the hands of different buyers, simply because one buyer may be able to do more with it than another.

There may be a buyer who has other businesses or operations which would "integrate" well with this company. The combination of operations may result in certain advantages or "synergies", so that one plus one equals more than two. For example, duplicated or overlapping aspects of the two companies may be eliminated, producing special efficiencies. Or certain competitive advantages may result. What ever the particular benefits, the company will be worth more to this buyer than to another, and he is apt to be willing to pay more for it as a result.

In addition, an acquisition agreement contains

many terms other than price, and each term has a value to one party or the other which can be translated into a certain monetary value. Gaining a certain term which you particularly want often requires that you trade off something else in exchange, and that trade-off may be in the form of a greater (or lesser) price paid or received for the company.

For example, two of the ways that you can buy a company are
   1- to purchase its assets* (buy the property owned by the company which is used to
   carry on its business), or
   2- to purchase its stock (buy ownership of
   "company" which owns the assets).

A purchase of assets is generally the more advantageous way for a buyer to purchase a company. One reason is because the buyer of assets does not take on any of the liabilities (or potential liabilities) of the selling company. It is also a bit easier for the asset buyer to obtain stepped up depreciation* on those assets. (Generally a new corporation is formed by the buyer to actually buy and hold those assets and carry on the business.) But a sale of stock (simply transferring the ownership of the original corporation) is generally more advantageous to the seller, due to the better capital gain tax treatment he gets on the sale proceeds. In each case the benefit can be translated into a rough dollar value, and the party who forfeited his particular advantage, by agreeing to the form of transaction which benefited the other party, generally expects something in return. Chapter 14 discusses other factors which can increase or decrease the sale price in this way.

In any event, the only thing that brings any buyer and seller to agreement on price is the strength of their relative desires to buy and sell that company. As mentioned earlier, your valuation figure is only your starting point for negotiation. However, by using a number of methods and thereby having a <u>range</u> of values to consider, you will have a good idea of what price ought to be your bottom line, and what might be the upper limit.

Using The Valuation To Find Out Whether An Acquisition Is "Doable"

A buyer needs to predict the price which might have to be paid for a company early on, in order to get an idea of whether the acquisition will even work out financially. The buyer is generally going to have to borrow the money needed to pay the purchase price, and the company will be expected to generate the cash flow* needed to make the payments on that loan.

The buyer will analyze the company's recent financial statements and from them determine what the available cash flow is likely to be for the next year. If it is not sufficient to pay the loan installments, with a healthy margin of cash flow left over for safety, then the deal is a waste of time to consider. But if the price the seller is asking is not out of line with the maximum feasible price according to this analysis, then the buyer knows that it is worthwhile to proceed with negotiations. A valuation helps tell him the limitations of the deal, and when it becomes apparent that the seller rigidly expects more than that, the buyer knows to walk away from it.

If this kind of cash flow analysis is required in your case, see Chapter 15 for instructions on how to do it. Cash flow analysis is so important to the determination of whether the deal makes sense, and is so closely related to some valuation procedures, that the two might as well be done together in most cases.

Using A Valuation To Help Borrow Money

If you are a buyer, your valuation will also be valuable to you when you meet with lenders, so that you can help justify the amount you are asking to borrow. For this purpose alone, however, a valuation is not generally worth the effort, because lenders are generally just going to focus on whether the collateral value of the company's assets cover the loan amount safely (see Chapter 13, on Secured Loan Value) and whether the business can produce enough cash to make the payments, with a large margin left over for safety

(See Chapter 15).

Valuation Brings You "Down To Earth" On Price

    It is important for a seller to be realistic about price. This is understandably difficult, because of the strong personal attachment an owner naturally has for a company which he has nutured for many years. But most of those in the buying arena are sophisticated enough financially to recognize the limitations of the company's worth, or else they get good outside advice on such matters. And buyers tend to be very disciplined when it comes to not overpaying for acquisitions. In addition, lenders are very conservative in this regard and do everything they can to recognize and avoid financing situations where the buyer might be overpaying. Otherwise the deal runs the risk of being under-secured and the cash-flow stretched more thinly than is necessary, all of which increases the risk involved for the lender and the buyer. All-in-all, the chances of actually receiving a price in excess of the company's real worth is fairly minuscule, so the entire process ends up to be a waste of everyone's time, particularly that of the seller.
    Perhaps more importantly, however, sellers who insistently pursue such a course suffer a loss of

credibility in the business community. Once an owner has been receptive to acquisition offers, even on a very informal basis, and the price expected is unrealistic, word tends to get out very quickly. The company will remain unsold for a long period of time, and thereby gain a shopworn, undesirable appearance to genuine prospective buyers. When the day comes that the owner does finally get serious about selling and comes down to earth on price, he will be at a serious disadvantage by having created a dubious impression of both himself and his company in the eyes of buyers and lenders. Still, it is not unusual to encounter a seller who maintains the notion that most acquirers have more money to spend than they know what to do with, or that selling-out is their way to "make a killing".

Although there are occasional exceptions, whenever a company is sold for what seems to be an outrageous price, it was probably worth it. You can also bet that a valuation study bore out that fact. Ironically, however, the caution of both buyers and lenders seems to go to the wind when the deal is extremely large, as may sometimes be the case in the more widely publicized mergers.

Sometimes bidding wars between competing buyers will drive up the price of an extremely attractive and highly promising company. However, these "auctions" are very rare in the case of a smaller company. For one thing, they are very difficult to orchestrate. For another, most buyers consider them a distasteful way of carrying out the sale of a business, and they flatly refuse to participate. In fact, most serious buyers consider it a matter of policy and propriety that they have the exclusive attention of the seller while they formulate their offer. The seller is generally given a very brief period within which to either accept or reject the delivered offer, or to negotiate different terms, and that is it. If there is agreement, the buyer will demand that the company is taken off of the market immediately, and there will be a written memorandum to that effect. The reason for this procedure is that the buyer does not want his offer "shopped around" to other interested parties as a price they will have to beat. The use of a buyer's offer in this way is considered extremely unethical. Most buyers who discover this being done will immediately withdraw from the deal and walk away for good.

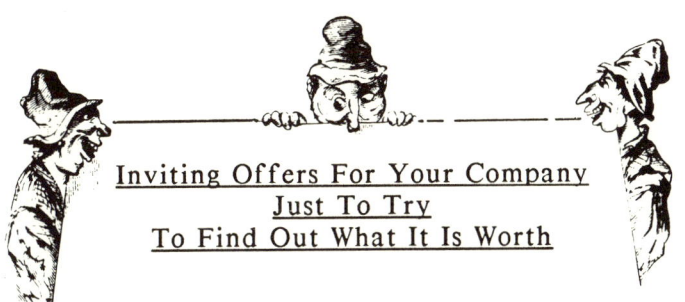

Inviting Offers For Your Company Just To Try To Find Out What It Is Worth

Sometimes an owner of a company will let it appear to buyers that the firm may be available for acquisition, without any real committed intention of selling, merely to invite offers and try to see what it might be worth. This only demonstrates very bad faith. Serious buyers spend a lot of time and a lot of money evaluating an acquisition prospect. An owner who engages in this practice is not only dishonest, he is hurting the interested buyer in a very real way. Besides, most interested parties will see through such a motive prior to the point where they actually deliver a real offer, and they will walk away at that point. All the "seller" will have succeed in doing is leaving a bad impression in the business community. Again, word gets out.

If the parties do somehow get into serious price discussions, those numbers are going to be significantly different from what a fully negotiated price would turn out to be. Relying on the figures discussed during the preliminaries as an indication of value is not wise. Besides, how can the seller proceed intelligently with price negotiation on any level without first conducting a valuation study as preparation? Any way you look at it, a complete valuation is essential.

NOTES:

CHAPTER 2
GETTING READY

<u>Learn As Much As You Reasonably Can About The Company</u>

The first thing you must do in assessing the value of a company is to learn as much about it as possible, without going overboard. Obviously, you could study any company for months before you really understood it. But your goal here is just to get the detailed financial information you need, plus enough other input to be able to refine that data and assess the level of risk associated with investment in the company. This chapter tells you exactly what questions to ask.

The reason for this in depth knowledge becomes more apparent as you get farther into your project. For example, it was mentioned in the prior chapter that there are many points throughout the valuation study when you are called upon to exercise your personal judgment to interpret or adjust a bit of data. To be able to do this, you must be familiar with the "context" for that number - why it is what it is. Your goal in adjusting data is only to present a clearer picture of the financial situation, never to misrepresent. Only when the data, as it currently stands, would paint a misleading picture, do you adjust it. Whenever data is adjusted, an explanation is mandatory, and you must understand what is going on in order to a have a plausible reason for what you have done. You've got to be knowledgeable about this company.

Chapter 3 of the manual explains how to adjust financial statements. The point being stressed here is that you will not know if something warrants explanation or adjustment unless you are thoroughly familiar with the company. You will not know when to question something or when to probe further. When you know all you should, your judgment will be about as good as an outsider's could be on most things.

Since it's tough to get everything you need in a single meeting, make sure you have established a contact within the company who you can call whenever you have a question. Warn that person that you will have a lot of them, and that you may make quite a pest of yourself. Then fire away and don't be bashful. Never worry about how dumb your questions sound. This process is essential in order to understand both the company's present financial picture and its future potential.

Make sure you take the right approach to securing this information, otherwise it can become quite an ordeal. The owners of a private company often perceive your requests as threatening intrusions into their personal affairs. This is natural, for up until now the business was just a personal matter of theirs and no one else really had any right to know the details regarding it. But a prospective buyer is entitled to all of the facts, and a valuator or intermediary can't do his job without them. So be diplomatic and show some understanding for the owner's sensitivity on this, but nonetheless be direct and straightforward from the start about the necessity of having all this input.

Explain up front what you will need and why you need it. It helps to give the person a copy of your checklist, and then give him a few days to prepare.

Offer the owner complete confidentiality, and then make sure you observe your promise. Treat the matters you are now privy to as you would expect them to be treated if it was your business. As an outsider, you may find it frustrating to try to get all of the information you need, but hang in there. Make sure the responsible parties understand that you can not proceed until you have it all.

Information
Checklist:

Although you may discover additional information that you want later, the following checklist will give you basically what you need. You may want to photocopy these pages and use them as a checklist in your meetings.

1- Income statements and balance sheets for the past 5 years.
- Make sure the income statements include detailed breakdowns of the individual categories of expenses, liabilities, and sources of income.
- Make sure the accompanying notes of the accountant are included.

2- All business activities engaged in.
- Products or services
- Separate operations
- Breakdown of sales for each product or separate operation.
- Retail sales
- Distribution
- Business cycles
- Other factors affecting business

3- Get detailed list of the company's individual assets*, including information on each one regarding:

- Date acquired
- Original cost
- Depreciation* taken to date
- Condition
- Whether obsolete
- Whether "general use" property, or designed for a specialized process.
- Equipment leased

4- Projected "capital expenditures*" for the next 5 years. (All improvements, equipment, or assets which the company will foreseeably have to purchase during the course of the next 5 years in order to stay competitive and keep operating at present levels.)

5- Inventory, broken down as follows (giving the original cost or book value* for each):

- raw materials
- work in progress (WIP)
- finished product
- obsolete inventory

Make sure you find out whether or not inventory is at its normal operating level. If not, find out what that level should be for each of these categories of inventory.

6- Get any appraisals available on the value of the assets.

7- Sales projections for the next several years.
(Remember that you are valuing the company as it stands now, not based on how it might perform in the future. However, such projections help you determine the degree of risk associated with the company. The greater or less the risk, respectively, the less or more a buyer

8- Market information concerning the particular products involved:

- Total size of the market (total annual sales by all companies)
- Projected growth of the total market in the future.
- What % of the total market is sold by the company ("market share")
- New developments and trends in the market and the products

(Much of this information can be obtained from industry associations, or the publishers of that
industry's trade magazines.)

9- Amount of accounts receivable*, including agings* as follows:

- 30 days old - current dollar amount
- 60 days old -   "
- 90 days old -   "
- 120+ days old -   "
- Number of customers with balances
- Credit terms extended to customers

10- Amount of accounts payable*, including agings* as follows:

- Current amount of payables owed on payment terms of 15 days or less:
    - Amount past due:
    - Average number of days past due:
- Current amount of payables owed on payment terms of 30 days or less:
    - Amount past due:
    - Average number of days past due:
- Current amount of payables owed on payment terms of 31 days or more:
    - Amount past due:
    - Average number of days past due:

11- The competition: who are they, what are their products, what are their estimated sales, what geographic areas do they serve?

   -What distinguishes this company from the competition?

12- Employees:
   - Breakdown by category
   - Number and average wage/salary level - for past three years
   - Benefits and incentives
   - Is there an agreement with a union?

13- Top 10 customers, with annual dollar volume of sales to each, and how long each has been a customer.

14- Weak points in the company, and improvements possible.

15- Explanations for any fluctuations in the company's performance over the past 5-10 years.

16- Marketing and sales:
   - How are sales conducted?
   - Factors emphasized in making sales (service, price, quality, delivery, etc.)
   - Areas avoided and reasons therefor
   - Areas emphasized and reasons therefor
   - Advertising - and theme
   - Other promotional techniques employed
   - Any relationship between location of facilities and market

17- Description of management structure and key individuals involved.

  - If the company is to be sold, will management stay afterwards?

18- Pending or threatened law suits

19- Leases and contracts (get copies or essential terms thereof)

20- Capitalization   (See balance sheet - for year ending:_____)

  - Short term debt:
    - Accounts payable
    - Accrued expenses
    - Income taxes payable
    - Other taxes payable
    - Interest payable
    - Short term loans - outstanding balance payments, interest rate, and terms.
  - Long term debt: Balance, monthly payments, interest rate, collateral for loan, lender.
  - Stock or Equity: Type of security, number of shares, owners, par value.

21- Company history
    - Include major plant expansions, product additions, acquisitions, and other milestones.

22- Pricing: method used and reasoning behind it.
    - Get product list and price schedule.
    - Effect of cost increases.
    - Price protection afforded to company by customers, and to customers by company.

23- Facilities - for each property:

- Owned or leased
- Size of site and size of building
- Age, condition, and type of construction.
- Expansion potential
- Percent of total production capacity being used

24- Names of each major supplier, including:
- Date started doing business with company
- Volume in previous year
- Type of products supplied
- Terms
- Quality of relationship
- Number of backup suppliers for those items

25- Insurance, fire, and police protection
- Insurance coverage and premium for each

Talk To Owners
and Managers For
Further Information

After you have gathered all of this information, you should have a good sense of the present state of health of the company, and the risk involved in the business. The next step is to talk to those who manage it to determine the following:

1- Where things could be tightened up and how much.

2- Potential sources of future sales growth, and what it would cost to develop them, including:
- New customers and new geographic market areas
- New products or departments within the company
- Possible enlargements of the sales and marketing staffs

3- Possible acquisitions of other businesses.

4- Excessive salaries, perquisites, and other generous benefits which could be scaled down. Also, any personal expenses of the owners being paid for and written off by the company as "business expenses".

5- Any unusual accounting or bookkeeping treatments being used by the company. Anything out of the ordinary which might cause the income statement or balance sheet to appear different than they would normally otherwise be in the case of another company.

6- External factors affecting the company, including:
- The state of the nation's economy, interest rates, and inflation levels.
- Technological developments in their field.

- Developments in other related fields which might have an impact.
- Population growth and movement.
- Changes in consumer tastes or demands.

This information will give you some insight into the company's future potential. If part of your job is also to project the future performance of the company, this input is essential. In that case, you will need to translate the effect of each of the foreseeable changes into a probable dollar result, and then create a new income statement showing the combined financial effect of all these changes. This is known as a "pro forma*" income statement. For anyone considering the purchase of a business, these predictions are an essential part of the analysis. Most buyers need to have reason to feel that they can do more with the company than the people before them have. However, given the uncertainty inherent in the business world, pro forma predictions are nothing to count on, and the acquisition had better make sense even if none of the proposed changes work out as expected.

This input from management is also important because it forms the basis for many of the "adjustments" you may have to make to the income statements, in order to compensate for the misleading effect on net profit produced by such things as unusually high salaries and unusual accounting treatments revealed by these questions. A "pro forma" statement should not be the basis for a valuation, but the use of an "adjusted" statement is acceptable if the changes made to the statement are justified by the facts. See Chapter 3 for instructions on how to adjust income statements.

After you have gathered all this information, proceed to Chapter 4 to determine which valuation methods to use in the particular case you are dealing with.

NOTES:

CHAPTER 3

FIRST: ADJUST THE FINANCIAL STATEMENTS

An "adjusted" income statement is an income statement* which has had certain figures in it changed. The changes are made in order to compensate for any unusual spending or accounting which would supposedly not exist if the company was in someone else's hands. The purpose is to show what the income statement would really look like if the company was being operated in the "normal" fashion by a corporate buyer. Balance sheets are also adjusted in some cases.

Why Financial Statements Are Adjusted

The goal in preparing an Adjusted Financial Statement is to produce an income statement which shows the actual present earning power of the company. It should reflect what you think earnings will be over a 12-month period beginning now.

37

An Income Statement* usually takes the following basic form:

Gross Sales
      (-) sales returns, customer allowances,
          and discounts
= Net Sales
      (-) Cost of Goods Sold

= Gross Profit
      (-) Operating Expenses - Including:
          - Depreciation*
          - Sales and Delivery Expenses
          - Administrative & General Expenses
            (including executive salaries)

= Operating Income
      (-) Interest and Other Financial Expenses

= Net Operating Income Before Tax

    A publicly-held corporation likes to show as large a "bottom-line" profit on its books as possible, in order to please its stockholders. But the aim of the private company is usually to show as small a bottom-line profit on its income statement as possible. It isn't that the private company wants to make less money. It wants to make all the money it can, but at the same time show that as little of it as possible is net income, which is taxable. As you undoubtedly know, that amount of income which remains after all of the business expenses of the year are deducted is taxed by the government. Therefore, if you can pay an expense through the company, with the money it earns before taxes, and thereby reduce the <u>taxable</u> net income which the company shows, you will generally be better off than if you paid the expense out of your own pocket with after-tax dollars.

    In the typical private company, many expenses of the owners are paid for in this way. In most cases, what businessmen do in this regard is neither dishonest nor illegal and the expenses are viewed by IRS as legitimate, deductible business expenses which benefit the company in some way. (Consult your accountant and the tax laws.) However, the valuator wants to view the company as if it was being operated as a subsidiary by another corporation which has no interest in bestowing these excess benefits upon the local managers. In using any valuation method, it is important that your figures are taken from an income statement which has been adjusted to exclude these unusual expenses.

Whenever an income statement has been adjusted, it is essential to disclose that fact to anyone receiving the valuation results. The "before" and "after" income statements should both be included in the report, as well as detailed notes on what has been adjusted and why. To overlook this would be dishonest. Not only that, but you may also have made some errors in judgment about how certain expenses ought to be adjusted. In that case, others need to have the opportunity to replace your revised figures with their own.

This is not a time for wishful thinking. Do not try to disguise real problems in the business. Your statement will be scrutinized carefully if a deal is undertaken, and it will only destroy your credibility, and perhaps the transaction, if you are misleading or unrealistic.

What To Adjust And How To Adjust It

1- Unusually generous salaries drawn by the owner/managers:
  - Any net income made by a corporation is taxed at a corporate rate. What is left over is called "retained earnings". These funds are either kept by the company or distributed to the owners (stockholders)

as their share of the profits from the business. The funds distributed to the shareholders are called "dividends". Once in the hands of the individual owner, this income is taxed again, this time at the owner's personal income tax rate, just like any other income he or she receives. To avoid this double taxation, owners who work in the business pay themselves management salaries which are as large as possible. (The IRS does provide some loose guidelines for figuring what the maximum "reasonable" salary might be.) When paid as salaries, these sums are deductible business expenses of the company, and therefore they are not taxed at the corporate level, only at the personal level.

  - Ask yourself what salary a parent corporation would normally pay a hired manager to do that same job. Subtract the excess salary from that section of the income statement which includes management salaries. You may have to add salary if the owner is underpaying himself relative to what a typical well-compensated professional manager is paid.

2- Company cars:
  - Following the same general reasoning behind high salaries, it often costs less to have your company pay for your car and write it off as a business expense than it does to pay for it out of your own pocket with dollars that have already been taxed twice.

  Ask yourself if providing an automobile to that employee is something a large corporation would do. If not, scratch the expense from the income statement.

- Don't forget to also exclude related expenses, such as auto insurance, gas, repairs, parking, etc.

3- Life insurance premiums:
- Small companies often pay the premiums for an owner-manager's life insurance. If the company itself is the beneficiary of the policy, it is probably because that person's particular talents and abilities are essential to the firm's success, and it would be very expensive to go out and find an equally able replacement for him if he were to die. However, the insurance would be able to pay for this if it happened. Although not tax deductible, this a legitimate expense, and it will continue to be if the covered individual plans to stay on board as an employee after any planned acquisition of the company. In that case, leave the expense on the income statement.

- If the beneficiary of the policy is another owner, then the purpose of the insurance is probably to allow that other owner to buy out the insured's share of the company upon the latter's death. This is so that the deceased's relatives don't inherit the stock and upset the company by trying to run it in a different way. In this case, the expense should be taken out.

-If someone else is the beneficiary of the policy, chances are it's just part of the employee's compensation package. It should be taken out of the statement if it would not be part of the expected compensation of a replacement manager.

4- Travel and Entertainment Expense ("T&E"):
- Often owners will write off country club dues, boats, vacations, resort properties, meals, and other extravagances as business expenses. This may be completely legitimate for the private owner, but the question you want to ask is: what is the realistic amount of travel and entertainment expense a corporate parent would allow an employee to spend to promote that business? It may be less than you think. Larger companies prefer to promote their business in other ways.

- On the other hand, travel expenses which are not associated with entertainment (for example, on a sales trip) are usually beyond question.

5-   Relatives employed within the business:
   - This technique is often used as a way to take more money out of the business in the form of <u>deductible</u> employee wages (so the money is not also taxed at the corporate level). The "employee" may be overpaid for the work done. But the primary benefit to the owner flows from the fact that the income received is reported on the separate personal income tax return of someone who is probably in a much lower tax bracket than the owner. If you pay yourself a $220,000 per year salary, it will be taxed at the highest rate (currently 50%). If you split that total amount up between several family members filing separate returns, it will be spread out and taxed at lower bracket rates.
 You will have much more left after taxes.
   The combined result is that this is one of the least expensive ways to take money out of the company, due to the reduced tax bite. To adjust, simply ask whether that employee is necessary, and, if so, whether they would normally be paid that much.

6-   Some other things to watch out for:

   - Legal, accounting, or other professional fees which are billed to the business as company expenses. These may actually be personal expenses of the owners.

- Interest paid to owners for loans they have made to the company. Were the loans necessary? Was the interest paid above market interest rates?

- Rent money paid by the company to the owners. Where the owners purchase real estate or equipment and the lease it to the company, simply ask whether the rent being paid is more than the company would pay if it rented from someone else. Otherwise, there is nothing wrong with these arrangements. They make good business sense.

- Any dramatic increase or decrease in a particular expense from one year to another. Look into the reason for it. It may reveal something unusual.

- Research & Development expenses. This label has been used by some companies to write off gifts and other ordinarily non-deductible expenditures made by a company for the benefit of particular individuals.

- "Unrelated" income or expenses. Remove from the statement any <u>non-operating</u> income or expenses. This includes any income or expenses which do not directly result from the primary business operations of the company. It is usually referred to on the statement as "other income" or "other expenses". Interest is usually an "other expense", so it should be deducted from the statement if it results from obligations which are not expected to continue in the future, or if it is otherwise not directly related to the primary business operations. "Other income" might include such things as income from property rental, investments, or other sources which have little or nothing to do with the business operations being evaluated. To allow these items to remain on the statement would be to give the misleading impression that the additional income is derived from the production and sale of the products or services which are the normal business of the company.

- Depreciation*. Remember that depreciation is an "operating expense" (See the Glossary definition for "Income Statement") which is usually included in either "Cost of Goods Sold" or "Administrative and General Expenses" on the income statement. If you are relying on income statements from past years to do your valuation, and you are anticipating an acquisition which will take the form of a sale of assets rather than a sale of stock (see Chapter 14), you will have to calculate a new depreciation figure to replace the old one, because the amount of depreciation taken in the past will not be the same as that which will be taken in the future. This is because, under the tax laws, when the buyer purchases those assets, he will be entitled to a fresh depreciation schedule for them, based on their cost. On the other hand, if he buys the company by purchasing its stock, he inherits the present depreciation schedule for those assets, and that depreciation may be mostly used up. (Although there is a way around this, using Section 338 of the tax code. See your accountant.) Depreciation increases your "cash flow*", and since most buyers of privately-held companies need the boost in cash flow provided by higher depreciation in order to make the acquisition work out financially, the majority of acquisitions involving companies with older (more fully depreciated) assets take this form. Prospective sellers of such a company should bear this is mind and expect to have to go this route if they want to make their deal, and adjust depreciation accordingly when conducting their own valuation. In this case you add the old depreciation figure back into the statement, and then deduct your new anticipated post-acquisition depreciation expense. <u>Go to Step 3 of Chapter 6</u> (Discounted Cash Flow Method) for instructions on how to do this.

- Non-recurring circumstances which have affected earnings positively or negatively in the current year. Remember that these won't exist under normal circumstances, so adjust their effect out of the statement.

- Certain unusually high or low balance sheet items in a particular year. If, for example, accounts receivable are much lower in one year than they are in most other years, you will want to find out why. If it is because something out of the ordinary has been done, you will want to adjust for it on the balance sheet. Particularly scrutinize inventory levels.

Since the appropriate adjustment is often difficult to accurately estimate in these cases, ask the company's controller or regular accountant what the figure would normally be, at that level of sales.

In most cases, the way you <u>compare</u> the different balance sheet items from year to year is as a percentage of total assets (if the item is on the asset side of the balance sheet). This means you divide the dollar amount of the item by the dollar amount of total assets for that year. This will give you a percentage. Do the same for the other years and then compare them. If the item is on the other side of the balance sheet (in Liabilities or Stockholders Equity), then compare it to its level in other years as a percentage Total Liabilities plus total Stockholder's Equity.

- Amounts which the seller indicates were skimmed from cash (implying that the profits are actually higher to that extent) may not materialize upon audit by a buyer's accountant. It is best not to rely upon such statements. Instead, only use figures which are verified by income tax returns.

Note on Adjusting Interest Expense:

In some of the methods described in this book, you are instructed to adjust the interest expenses. You are told to add back any interest expenses that would not exist after the company was purchased by an acquirer. You are also told to deduct from income the amount of interest that a purchaser would be expected to incur as a result of financing the purchase price.

Although you may not be conducting your valuation with a view toward selling the company, you must remember that, as a rule, "value" is that amount that something would bring if it were sold, and it must be determined with regard to the circumstances in which it would be sold. Therefore, except in very unusual cases, you will have to deduct this additional interest expense from income even if no sale is being planned. One such exception might be in the case of determining value for the purpose of a buy-sell agreement between partners or co-owners.

This will generally yield a more conservative valuation. For most non-acquisition purposes, this is more advantageous to the owner anyway. But one should note from all this that, depending on whether or not the additional interest expense is appropriate, it is possible to have two different valuations for the same company.

Note On Adjusting Partnership or Sole Proprietor Statements:

In the case of a partnership, there generally is no expense on the income statement for salaries paid to the partners. Usually they take out their part of the profits as a "draw". But in valuation, we always regard the business as a corporation, and on a corporation income statement there is always a deduction for all salaries paid. Therefore, it is necessary to determine what salary a paid manager in this post would normally earn and deduct that amount on the income statement.

Likewise, you will also have to assume that corporate income taxes are being paid. A partnership pays no income taxes itself. Only the partners pay income taxes, on their distributive share of the profits. So, determine what the corporate income tax would be if the income of the partnership had been earned by a corporation, and deduct it from the net income on the statement.

The same rules hold true in the case of a sole proprietorship (an unincorporated business with one owner).

Now you should have the idea. Just make sure you have a very detailed breakdown of all of the business expenses so that you can have a chance to spot these things. If it is your own company, you know right away what to adjust. If it is not your company, do not be afraid to ask about these items. Although it is a sensitive topic, you should assume that the owners have been acting ethically and should not mind answering honestly, providing they are assured of the confidentiality to which they are entitled. In fact, if the owners want to achieve as high a valuation as possible, then it is actually in their best interest to reveal these things to the valuator, since the expense added back will serve to increase the net income shown on the statement and, therefore, increase the apparent value of the company.

Notes:

CHAPTER 4

WHICH METHODS TO USE IN YOUR CASE

This section gives a brief description of each valuation method presented in this manual and instructs you on when each is used. Conduct your valuation using every method which seems to apply to your case. Then, at the end, compare your results according to the directions in Chapter 14. At that point you should be able to narrow the range of values and zero in on a specific number.

Ability-To-Pay Method   (Chapter 5)

When To Use: It is necessary to use this method in almost all cases.
- Buyers: Use it make sure the acquisition can pay for itself out of its own cash flow* if you will be borrowing the purchase price.
- Sellers: Use it to find the maximum price which the company's cash flow can support,

based on the assumption that this cash flow must be adequate to make the payments on the buyer's acquisition debt.

Brief Description: Here you are saying that the company will provide $X of cash flow to make debt payments - so, what purchase price does that mean a buyer can afford to pay if he has to make all of his payments out of that sum?
Project the annual net cash flow for 8 to 10 years. Find the average. Deduct average yearly Capital Expenditures* expected. The result is the Average Annual Cash Flow Available for Debt Service. Next, determine what size loan a buyer can take out to buy the company if he has this amount available for loan payments. Figuring that the loan amount will be 80-90% of the company's purchase price, determine what that purchase price will be.

Discounted Cash Flow Method   (Chapter 6)

When To Use:
- When the company is being purchased as an "investment" to be held for only a limited number of years (no more than 5 to 10).
- When the purchase is going to be financed by a much larger than normal proportion of debt in relation the cash invested in the deal ("highly leveraged"), and the purchasers will probable turn around and resell the company within 10 years.
- Any extremely risky situation.

Brief Description: For each year of the anticipated period during which the company will be held by the new owner, project the annual cash flow*. Deduct annual expected taxes, capital expenditures*, and debt service (loan payments). Compute the "present value*" of the remaining amount for each year. Add them together. Add to this the present value* of corporate assets expected to remain at the end of the entire period. Subtract liabilities expected to remain at the end of the period.

Capitalization of Income Stream Method   (Chapt. 7)

When To Use: Anytime a business produces after-tax earnings which are substantial enough to result in "goodwill* value" over and above the value of the company's assets.

Brief Description: An "adjusted" income statement is prepared to show the company's probable performance for the next 12 months. The net operating income after tax is divided by a factor which is equivalent to the rate of return an investor would currently expect from any other investment of equivalent risk. The resulting figure is reduced by the amount of any liabilities which the company's purchaser would assume in the transaction. The result is the value of the company.

Excess Earnings Method   (Chapter 8)

When To Use: To value any profitable company.

Brief Description: Assumes that a business is worth the market value of its tangible assets, plus a premium for "goodwill*" if the earnings are high enough.

Economic Value of Assets Method   (Chapter 9)

When To Use:
   - Whenever the Excess Earnings Method, or some other method, shows that the earnings of the company are not significant enough to warrant any "goodwill*" value.
   - To value any business with a stagnant, unsteady, or downward sales or earnings trend.
   - In any case where it appears that the business may bring its owners a higher price if it is broken up and its assets sold individually.

Brief Description: Assets are sold at market or liquidation value. Market value or liquidation value for each individual asset is determined by independent appraisal and the values are totaled. Do not use "replacement value" appraisals conducted for insurance purposes. Determine the value of any intangible assets* for which there is a resale market, and add to the total.

Net Worth Per Books Approach   (Chapter 10)

When To Use: Not really a valuation method. Used in price negotiations, only as a supplement to Economic Value of Assets Method. Net Worth, or total Book Value, is commonly viewed as a target price by buyers in leveraged buyouts* and corporate divestitures.

Brief Description: Total Assets minus Total Liabilities, using the figures given on the balance sheet.

Internal Revenue Service Method   (Chapter 11)

When To Use:
  - Primarily for estate and gift tax purposes.
  - For any situation where tax considerations
    of any type are in issue.

Brief Description: Add the value of the Net Tangible Assets* of the company (Total Assets, minus Intangible Assets*, minus Liabilities) to the capitalized value* of "excess earnings" (earnings in excess of the "normal return" which those tangible assets would have yielded to a typical company).

Comparable Sales Method   (Chapter 12)

When To Use: Should only actually be used when valuing a publicly-held company where adequate, detailed data on recent acquisitions of "similar" publicly-held companies is available. Such data should not be used to value a privately-held or closely-held company, but it can be valuable ammunition in the price negotiations for such companies.

Brief Description: Recent acquisitions of comparable companies are analyzed and the sales price of each is painstakingly adjusted to reflect what it would have been had that company been identical in all significant respects to the subject company. The price is then translated into the form of a "multiple" of after-tax earnings. This process is repeated for a large number of transactions, and the average of the resulting "multiples" is determined. The value of the subject company is arrived at by multiplying its own after-tax earnings by this average multiple.

Price/Earnings Ratio Method ("Multiple" of Earnings Method) (Chapter 12)

When To Use: Should only actually be used in valuing a publicly-held company. However, as with the Comparable Sales Method, the study can sometimes provide useful ammunition to support positions taken during the course of price negotiations for privately-held companies.

Brief Description: Find a group of publicly-held and traded companies which are similar to the one being valued. In each case, find the stock's current traded price and then divide it by the net after-tax earnings per share of that company reported on that same date. Find the average of all these "P/E Ratios". Multiply it times the net after-tax earnings of the subject company.

Replacement Cost Approach (Chapter 12)

When To Use: Only used for insurance purposes, and only then where the coverage is for the "replacement cost" of the insured property.

Brief Description: Generally, replacement cost for individual assets is estimated by a qualified independent appraiser. The replacement cost for the entire business would be the cost of recreating that business, in every respect, from scratch. However, this is an inappropriate measure of value for almost all situations, besides being almost impossible to accurately ascertain.

Rule-of-Thumb Pricing Methods Used For Particular Types Of Businesses (Chapter 12)

When To Use:
- When established industry practice dictates that businesses within it are customarily sold at prices determined according to this method, and you will probably be selling to a buyer who is already involved in that field and therefore will insist on relying upon it. In such cases, although it can often result in a misleading oversimplification, the buyer or seller may be stuck with it. Whenever possible, always rely more heavily on the other methods.

- Use as a rough measure for initial comparison of one business to another within the same industry.

Brief Description: Usually an industry accepted "factor" is multiplied times Gross Monthly Sales (or some other measure) in order to give the "value" of the business.

Secured Loan Value (Chapter 13)

When To Use: Only to determine how large an amount may be borrowed by using the company's assets as collateral or security for the loan. Must be referred to when using any other method which assumes the presence of new acquisition financing as part of the post-acquisition financial structure.

Brief Description: Multiply the accepted lending industry "advance rates" times the value of the assets. Different advance rates apply to different types of assets. Add up the results obtained for each category of assets to get the total Secured Loan Value.

After you have determined which methods to use, proceed to the appropriate Chapter for each and follow the step-by-step instructions. When you have completed them all, go to Chapter 14 for instructions on how to complete the study.

CHAPTER 5

THE ABILITY TO PAY METHOD

When To Use This Method

This method should be employed in almost all cases. The concept behind it is that a correct price to pay for a company is one that will provide the buyer with the ability to pay for the purchased business out of its own net cash flow over a reasonable length of time, with a reasonable cushion of cash left over each year as a margin for safety. If a company can not pay for itself over a reasonable length of time, then it is considered a bad price and a bad investment, no matter how low the purchase price was. This should always be one of the first valuation methods used. If you are a buyer, it will tell you whether it is okay to go forward on the deal. (It is very similar to the Discounted Cash Flow Method in that regard.)

Note: Just as with the Discounted Cash Flow Method in Chapter 6, this method requires you to "assume" a ball-park purchase price for the company in order to be able to go through the procedure. While it may appear absurd to have to guess at the purchase price in order to use a method for determining purchase price, that is exactly what is required in this case. What you do, in effect, is "back into" that price. With the price you calculate, you look to see if it verified your assumed price. If it didn't, you adjust your assumed price up or down according to how far off you were, and you try your calculations again. You usually have to go back and forth a few times until you have narrowed the gap sufficiently and the end result verifies your latest assumption.

For example, if you assume a purchase price in Step 3 of $4,000,000, yet your end result is a value if $6,000,000, you know you guessed too low, so try it again, compromising at $5,000,000. After a couple of tries, you will have narrowed it down. The same idea applies to Chapter 6, on the Discounted Cash Flow Method.

Obviously, if you have computer and a spreadsheet type program, this "what if" process becomes much easier. Once you set up the model with the basic figures, you can just plug in your revised assumptions on price and all the other figures will change automatically. But if you have to do your calculations manually, just remember that any valuation result is going to be inherently inexact anyway, and so getting the thing to match up right down to the dollar is not going to be worth the effort involved.

So that you have a better idea of what figure you should assume initially, it might be easier if you undertake some other applicable valuation methods first.

Limitation To This Method

This method is ideal for someone buying a business solely for its income. It is a must for a buyer who will expect the company to be completely independent financially, or if there is not going to be any special relationship or synergy resulting between it and other businesses of the buyer. But if the buyer is purchasing primarily to gain some business advantage which will result when the company is combined with other businesses operated by that buyer, then it should be worth it to him to have to dig into his pocket a little and pay a bit more than otherwise might be warranted.

In such a case, he might have to subsidize the loan payments to a small extent or put a little more cash into the deal. These "other advantages" we are talking about include such benefits as capturing a supplier, gaining new distribution channels, or tying down needed support services for other operations. However, merely adding to a product line, providing additional sales staff (they may end up combined anyway), or adding production capability does not normally produce the kind of advantage that would justify a higher price than the company can reasonably pay for out of its own cash flow. In addition, to make this assumption, you have to know who your buyer is, and that is something which is often impossible to predict.

Because this method makes so much sense, it is very useful in negotiating the price back to a reasonable level when the seller's expectations have become unrealistically high. On the other hand, if you are a seller, you want to try to argue that there are special advantages which will result to the particular buyer from the acquisition, and that these justify a higher price.

Brief Description of the Method

As stated above, with this method you "back into" the price. Basically, you calculate the final after-tax dollars which are available for debt payments. Of this amount, 20% to 50% is reserved as a safety cushion. The remainder is the "amount available for annual debt service". Once you break this down to available monthly payments, you can figure out the loan amount which these monthly payments correspond to, and that amount leads you to your price. See the "Summary" at the end of this chapter for a picture of this method.

Remember: The reason for the cushion requirement is not only to insure that the company can meet its debt service safely, but also to make sure that there is a reasonable profit for the buyer. If all the buyer ends up doing is taking on a load of debt with no current return, then the investment has limited value for him. Growth in sales and earnings in future years is always speculative, so an increase in the value of the underlying investment is nothing to count on by itself. The buyer must have an attractive return in exchange for his time, effort, and financial investment.

Assumptions To Make: A reasonable period for the business to pay for itself in is 8 to 10 years. If you lack a better estimate of the holding period for the investment, use ten years, and figure that any term loans taken out to finance the acquisition will be repaid by or at the end of that period. Ten years seems to be a term that lenders like. For assumed interest rates, use prime rate plus 2 to 3 points, depending on the condition of the company. Assume that the purchase price is 80% borrowed (75% to 85% is average).

Steps:

1- Predict Net Sales for each of the next ten years (or for the period of time you have chosen as that within which the business must have paid for itself). Do not use more than ten years. Calculate the average of these figures.

Note On Predictions For Increased Future Sales or Profits: Although a buyers are free to speculate on the possibility of improved sales and earnings in their personal evaluation of the company, such figures are not taken into consideration for valuation purposes, nor are they taken into account by lenders who may consider financing the deal. Increased profits from tighter financial controls and other cost-cutting measures may be feasible, but they are still too speculative to actually rely upon. To buyers and lenders, the company must be able to stand on its own as it is now, and the deal will always be structured so that post-acquisition financial improvements will be hoped for but not essential to the success of the deal. Especially where current management will stay, the company is assumed to be operating at maximum efficiency. Therefore, in projecting net sales, you must look to the sales figure for the last full reported year and assume that the same level of sales will continue in the future, increased at <u>most</u> each year by a <u>conservative</u> rate of inflation (4% to 6%). If annual sales have fluctuated greatly during recent years, then use a "weighted average"* of annual sales for the last five years instead of using last year's figure. See the Glossary for instructions on how to calculated a weighted average*.

When might the seller be justified in assuming greater annual sales growth than this?: Only in the case where the actual historic sales trend shows that revenues have consistently increased, without exception, for a significant number of years (at least ten), and that such sales have increased by a steady and predictable annual rate. There must be no known instabilities in the market or the customer demand. The market must be one that is relatively immune to external economic influences (such as rising interest rates or recession), to changes in demographic patterns, or to similar uncontrollables. The product or service must not be one which is subject to significant technological change or other advancements, such that it may become outdated by the development of new products, or else threatened competitively by vastly improved ones. As you can see, very few companies are going to meet these criteria, so it is actually a rare case when increasing future sales can be reliably assumed.

2- Determine the Operating Profit* before tax.

a- In general, look to the historic (last year's) performance and assume that the same Net Operating Income (or Profit) will continue in the future. If you are a buyer, you do not want to try to tighten up on the expenses on the statement in order to raise the Operating Income. If you acknowledge the feasibility of these changes, this may serve to justify a higher price. You may even see expenses which would need to be added if you take over the company.

b- If you are a seller, do what you can to argue for a higher price by going back over the income and expenses statement and scrutinizing it. Tighten up expenses wherever honest, obvious improvements can be made, and eliminate excess salary and perks. This will yield an "Adjusted Income Statement", the preparation of which is treated more thoroughly in Chapter 3 of this manual.

c- Whatever figures you choose to work with, determine what percentage of net sales the pre-tax operating profit is. (To get this, divide Net Operating Income by Net Sales.) Then multiply the Average Annual Net Sales figure calculated in Step 1 by this percentage. This will give you the average anticipated net operating income of the company during the projected period of years.

NOTE: If there has been a great deal of fluctuation over the past several years in the Operating Income, then use a "weighted average"* of the Percentage Operating Profits* from the past five years. See the Glossary for instructions on how to calculate a weighted average*.

3- Calculate the Net Operating Income After Tax.
To do this, subtract your anticipated future tax deductions for Interest and Depreciation* from the Operating Income determined in Step 1, and apply the corporate income tax rates to the result:

a- First determine the deduction for Interest Expense. For this you must assume a ball-park purchase price, and then assume that your loan will be for an amount equal to 80% of it. Assume a 10 year term for the loan, with interest at prime rate plus 2 to 3 percent. Determine the total amount of all loan payments to be made over the entire ten year term, then subtract the principal amount of the loan. This give you the total amount of interest which will be paid. Divide by 10 years to get the average annual interest.

Note: If you are a buyer, you may have to spend a lot more money to take over this company than just the purchase price. You may need a new facility if a lease is lost. You may need to replenish inventory which has been allowed to deplete before the sale. You will need money for working capital. In this case, your interest figure should reflect the entire amount of borrowing necessary, not just the part needed for the purchase price. This often involves several different loans, not just one larger loan. Step 4 of Chapter 6 discusses this subject of loan structure and how to calculate probable future interest payments in more detail. Refer to it now if the single loan approach assumed above is too simple for your situation.

b- Next, determine the amount of the deduction for Depreciation*. Depreciation has already been deducted from operating income on the income statement (as an operating expense). However, if the sale of the company is likely to take the form of a sale of assets, rather than a sale of stock, the depreciation amount formerly taken will not apply anymore. You will have to replace it with the different depreciation amount which will be allowed to the new corporation set up by the buyer for the purpose of purchasing those assets and carrying on the business of the company.

The majority of transactions involving privately held* companies are structured as asset purchases. Part of the reason is because most buyers seem to feel that this is the easiest way for them to get increased depreciation*. The purchase price is allocated to the individual assets, and is regarded as their individual "cost" to the buyer. This replaces the old original cost being depreciated, which has been depleted through several years' of deductions. Buyers need increased depreciation is because it gives them greater cash flow*. The company only has so much cash flowing through it to work with, and if they can increase that amount, then they will have more to make loan payments with. For the seller, this means the buyer can afford a higher purchase price. The seller should usually be willing to go with a deal that accomplishes this.

It used to be that a deal carried out by a purchase of the company's stock required the buyer to keep using the old depleted depreciation schedule of the past. At the time of this writing there is a way around that, by using Section 338 of the Internal Revenue Code, which allows you to step up the depreciable tax basis of the assets. See your accountant for details.

To adjust depreciation, assume the same ball-park purchase price as used above in Step 3a, and allocate it as the buyer would to the various assets. (See "Allocation of Purchase Price" in the Glossary). Remember that allocation to goodwill* is usually meager, if not non-existent, even where goodwill may exist.

Then figure the amount of annual depreciation for each class of assets, and add them up. The rules do differ regarding the allowable amount of depreciation for different types of assets. Go to Step 3 of Chapter 6 (Discounted Cash Flow Method) for more complete instructions on how to do this, and consult the latest tax laws for up to date depreciation rules.

Once the anticipated future annual depreciation is arrived at, add the amount of depreciation formerly taken back into operating profit, and subtract the new depreciation figure. Now you should have the amount of Taxable Operating Income.

 c- Subtract Corporate Income Taxes (Federal and State): Use the corporate income tax rates. Get them from your accountant, the IRS and state tax authorities, or an up-to-date tax manual. Refer to Step 5 of Chapter 6 for more detail on how to calculate taxes.

 d- Add back the amount of any federal Investment Tax Credit available. This step may be more picky than necessary, but if you wish to go to the trouble then refer to Step 6 of Chapter 6 for more complete instructions on doing it.

e- Your result is the Average Projected Net Operating Income After Tax.

4- Add back the Interest and the Depreciation deducted earlier (in Step 3) to get Net Cash Flow After Tax.

Depreciation is added back here because it is a non-cash operating expense. That is, it is deducted on the income statement, but you haven't really shelled out any money to pay it. (You paid it when you bought the asset, but you were not allowed to deduct the entire amount at once in the year it was spent.) In any event, the actual amount of cash you have available is generally greater than the income statement shows, so you add it back to reflect this.

Interest is added back here because, below, in another step, you are going to deduct <u>total</u> debt service payments, which include both principal and interest together. You do not want to subtract interest twice.

5- From Net Cash Flow After Tax (step 4), deduct anticipated Average Annual Capital Expenditures* for the period.

Consult the company's management to find out what the total annual Capital Expenditures* have averaged in the past. Any expenditure or investment which is not written off <u>entirely</u> in the year in which it is actually made is generally a "capital expenditure". New equipment and improvements to real estate are the most obvious examples. Watch out for <u>deferred</u> capital expenditures which management may have allowed to pile up. These are necessary investments in plant, repairs, improvements, or equipment which should have been made but were not. These may result in extraordinary expenditures in the future. The same is true if advancing technologies will require investment in new processes or equipment in order to remain competitive.

If a historic average capital expenditures figure is chosen, remember to increase it by a factor for inflation (4% to 6%) for each year into the projected period. The actual costs for these things are always on the rise, just like everything else.

Add the annual capital expenditures figures together, and find the average. Subtract that from Net Cash Flow After Tax (from step 4). This will give you Net Cash Flow Before Debt Service.

6- Subtract an appropriate Cash Flow Safety Cushion from Net Cash Flow Before Debt Service.

Investors and lenders will demand a safety margin in the cash flow of between 20 and 50 percent, depending on their perception of the risk involved in the deal. The result is that only 50 to 80 percent of the cash flow is really available for debt payments. Try to be objective and conservative in guessing at the safety cushion which will be required.

Determine the amount remaining after the cushion is deducted, and divide that figure by 12 to show the available monthly loan payment.

7- Calculate what loan amount this monthly payment will support.

Assume a ten-year loan term and an interest rate equal to the current prime rate plus 2 or 3 percentage points, depending on the risk involved in the deal as reflected by the company's relative financial strength. For simplicity, in this method we generally assume that only one term loan is used to finance the purchase price even though several different types of loans (or "layers" of financing) may be used by the buyer. However, a revolving working capital* loan (a line of credit) will probably be required as well, in order to have some cash to operate the company. In that case, figure that the monthly <u>interest</u> payments which will be due on that loan must also be paid from this cash flow. (In most cases, only interest is absolutely required to be paid on such a loan. The principal is generally only repaid as excess earnings are available to do so, assuming the lender has confidence in the security for the loan and the reliability of the borrower.) <u>Un</u>secured debt payments must also be provided out of this cash flow, as well as preferred stock dividends.

<u>Note:</u> While traditional "loan tables" can be used to determine what loan amount corresponds to the

available monthly payment, the easiest way to find it is to use a financial calculator which carries out this function. Texas Instruments and Hewlett-Packard make some very nice models which also perform the present value* conversions required in other methods.

8- Knowing, from step 7, the amount of loan principal which can be borrowed to finance the purchase price, determine what the <u>total</u> purchase price will be.

Do this by assuming that 80% of the purchase price will be borrowed. Therefore, you divide the amount calculated in step 7 by .80 to get total price. Assume that in a riskier transaction the lenders are going to demand that more than 20% cash is put into the deal.

<u>Caution:</u> This method is very imprecise, and it should not be relied upon to validate the company's actual ability to meet debt payments or other obligations. For that, a year-by-year analysis of cash flow should be done in conjunction with the advice of qualified accountants. See Chapter 15 in that regard.

Summary:

    Average annual Net Sales (for the projected period) (Step 1)

X Operating Profit Percentage (Step 2)

= Average annual Net Operating Income anticipated during the period

(plus) interest deductions used in prior years
(minus) expected average Annual
       Interest Expense (Step 3a)
(plus) Depreciation deduction   } depreciation
       used in prior year   } adjusted in
(minus) actual future Depreciation } case of an
       deduction expected   } asset deal
                                   (Step 3b)

= Taxable Net Income

(minus) Income Taxes (Step 3c)

= Average projected Net Operating Income After Tax

(plus) Depreciation (Step 4)
(plus) Interest deducted above in Step 3a
      (Step 4)

= Net Cash Flow After Tax

(minus) Average Annual Capital Expenditures (Step 5)

= Net Cash Flow Before Debt Service

(minus) 20% to 50% Safety Cushion (Step 6)

= Net Cash Flow Available for Debt Service

Then, divide this amount by 12 to give the monthly loan payment available, and determine the principal loan amount which it will support.

CHAPTER 6

DISCOUNTED CASH FLOW METHOD

When To Use This Method

This method is really only used in situations where the buyer will be holding on to the business for a limited number of years (no more than about 10). Many "leveraged buyouts"* fall into this category, since they are often viewed as temporary investments by their purchasers. In any leveraged buyout, virtually all of the purchase price is borrowed, and the assets of the company are used as the loan collateral. Another common instance where the acquisition is not held long is where a troubled company is bought at a bargain price, put back on its feet, and resold at a higher price consistent with its improved performance (a "turnaround"*).

This method is also appropriate for any situation where there is a very high risk associated with the acquisition.

The method involves the same basic cash flow* analysis that any buyer has to go through in order to predict whether an acquisition is going to work out financially. He wants to make sure that the business will produce enough cash income to completely cover the payments on the acquisition debt, with room to spare for safety reasons. Any buyer should anticipate the need to do this sort of study, and if this valuation method has been completed beforehand, most of the work will already be done. The steps in this method may seem somewhat exhaustive, but this is so that the work will be complete enough to use later for cash flow analysis.

NOTE: Because Steps 3 and 4 of this method require you to assume a ball-park purchase price to start with, it is probably a good idea to undertake any other applicable valuation methods first, so that you have a better idea of what kind of figure to assume. Please refer to the "Note" in the beginning of Chapter 5 for a little more explanation on this.

Brief Description of the Method

See the "Summary" at the end of this chapter for a picture of the method. For each year of the projection, you should have a vertical row of figures in that form.

a- First you forecast the income and cash flow* of the company into the future for a given number of years. For each year, you then calculate the "present value"* of that cash flow figure.

b- You then add up the values of all the assets of the company which are expected to be present at the end of the projected period (the "residual assets"). Then calculate the present value of that figure also.

c- Then add up the present values of the cash flows for each year (step a), plus the present value of the assets expected to remain at the end of the whole period (step b), minus any debts or other liabilities expected to remain at the end of the period.

Steps:

1- Project Net Sales* for several years.

How many years? Pick the shorter of: ten years, the term of the longest piece of debt used to finance the acquisition, or the number of years within which the company will be resold.

It is important to be conservative, so do not assume that sales will be any higher in the first year following the acquisition than they are presently. No matter how confident you are about increased sales, they aren't there yet, and given the uncertainties inherent in business, they are nothing you can count on. Besides, the buyer is paying for the company as it stands now, not for what it has not yet become.

Assume the same level of sales in the first year as is present now, and assume that you can maintain that level in each subsequent year. If sales have fluctuated greatly in recent years, then use a weighted average* of the net sales for the last five years instead.

For each year after the first one, increase the sales figure over that of the prior year by an amount equal to a conservative rate of inflation (4% to 6%). What this does is assume that you will sell the same number of units (of what- ever it is you sell) in each year, but that the increasing costs of producing it will be passed on to the customer in the form of annual price increases. Essentially, it assumes flat sales.

Are you justified in anticipating higher future sales than this? Only in the case where the company has shown a consistent trend of annually increasing sales in every year for a very long period of time (say, 8 to 10 years). The sales must have climbed at a steady rate (for instance, 10% to 15% each year) and not in an unstable or volatile fashion (for instance, 5% in one year and 30% in the next). In other words, the increase must be reliably predictable. The market demand for the product or service must be stable and proven over many, many years. It must not be a product which is subject to any significant change in design or delivery (as is the case with products in which there are rapidly advancing technologies). The company must be relatively immune from external economic influences.

Only very mundane products generally fill this bill. But it's tough to assume increasing sales in a mundane field either. The markets for mundane products grow very slowly, and since the market share held by each company in a mundane field is firmly entrenched and hard to steal, you really can not safely assume increasing sales in a mundane product field either. Furthermore, be advised that any lenders thinking about financing the deal are going to assume that there will be no increase in sales, no matter what the past sales trends are. However, they may feel more secure about the risk involved with the loan if there is a positive sales trend. Therefore, stick with the flat sales presumption.

2- Determine "Operating Profit" for each year of the projected period.

First prepare an adjusted historic income statement. (See Chapter 3.) Then, multiply the "percentage operating profit"* from it times the net sales figure in each year of the projection (from Step 1). This will give you the "Operating Profit" for each projected year.

In other words, if operating profit (before tax) is 9.5% of the net sales figure on the adjusted statement, then assume that operating profit will be 9.5% of net sales in each year of your projection.

Where historic operating profit percentages for the company have fluctuated widely over the past several years, use their weighted average* for the last five years. See the Glossary for an explanation of how to find a weighted average.

Do not use the percentage operating profit from a "pro forma"* income statement for this. "Pro forma", in this case, refers to a speculative prediction of what you think the income statement is going to look like in the year after the acquisition and following certain changes and "improvements" made by the buyer. In most cases this should not be used as the basis for calculating purchase price, for one buys a company as it stands now, not as it "may" become in the future.

Pro forma income statements come into play for a buyer, for his own purposes, when he is trying to determine what he really thinks he can do with the company. He may also use them to help convince lenders and investors that they are making a good decision by sinking their money into the company. The risk that these results will actually be obtained rests entirely on him, and it is not really appropriate for a seller to attempt to base the current value of the company on predictions for future performance which exceed what the company is actually doing now.

The preparation and use of pro forma income statements is discussed more thoroughly in Chapter 15.

3- Adjust the operating profit figure for each projected year for any significant changes in depreciation* which will be taken in future years.

Depreciation is an expense which is deducted on the income statement before you get to Operating Income. If depreciation deductions in the post-acquisition years are expected to be much different from those taken in the year used for the adjusted income statement, then you must adjust the operating income for each of the projected years. How do you do that? By adding back into the operating income, in each projected year, an amount equal to the depreciation taken on the adjusted statement. Then you determine the actual depreciation that will be taken in those future years and subtract it. This replaces the old figure with the new figure.

If you anticipate a transaction in which the stock of the existing company will be purchased, then the buyer will inherit the company's present depreciation schedule. Since he will depreciate the company's assets as they have been in the past, no adjustment is necessary. In that case, go on to the next step.

However, where the assets of the company are older and most of their cost has already been written off, the buyer will generally want to structure a deal where he forms a new corporation to purchase the assets of the company (an "asset deal"). After the sale the selling company will then have a bunch of cash, but no hard assets and no business. It will wind down and "liquidate", distributing the cash to its stockholders. But now the new corporation can enjoy longer and higher depreciation writeoffs on those assets than the old

71

corporation could have with its old schedule. This improves the company's cash flow*. The total purchase price paid by the buyer is divvied-up among the assets which have been purchased ("allocation of purchase price"*), and the amount assigned to each is regarded as its "cost" for depreciation purposes. (Also referred to as its "tax basis".) The IRS allows different types of assets to be written off over different periods of time. This period is sometimes referred to as "useful life". Sometimes several different depreciation methods can be used for a single type of asset. But for our purposes here, assume that an equal portion of the cost of the asset is written off each year ("straight line method"). Look in a current tax guide or the tax code and find the number of years over which each category of assets can be depreciated. Then divide that number into the amount of purchase price allocated to them in order to get the annual depreciation allowed for that group of assets.

As an illustration, assume that you have paid $1000 for an asset, and that the tax laws say you can depreciate it. (Not all assets may be depreciated.) Assume the tax laws also tell you that this type of asset may be depreciated over 5 years on a "straight line" basis (equal amounts of depreciation taken each year). This means you can deduct $200 per year from your company's income in figuring taxable income.

So, go back to the old adjusted income statement and find out what amount was deducted in that year for depreciation. For each year of the projection, add that amount back into the operating profit calculated in Step 2. Then assume a ball-park purchase price and allocate it among the assets. Figure out what the new annual depreciation amount will be for each of those future years and deduct it from the operating profit in each year.

Consult an accountant or an up-to-date tax guide for the actual depreciation rules. They can be complex. For example, at the time of this writing, it is most common to write off real estate over 18 years on a straight-line basis. However, only part of the amount allocated to real estate is depreciable - that is the part which is allocated to the building itself and the equipment permanently attached to it (the fixtures). Land can not be depreciated, so the value of the lot must be subtracted before the calculation is made. Furthermore, there are generally some optional ways to depreciate anything, so ask your accountant for some guidelines, but try not to get too wrapped up in detailed calculations because you want to keep in mind the fact that your valuation results are going to be inexact anyway. However, whatever assumptions you make regarding depreciation, include notes with your work explaining what you have done. If your valuation will have decisive input, then your assumptions regarding such things as depreciation become more critical. Don't rely on your work for financial or legal decisions unless you have had an qualified accountant check over it, verify your conclusions, and submit additional advice.

Remember that it is the buyer who will usually have most of the say regarding how the purchase price is allocated, but that both buyer and seller will be bound by it for tax purposes. The allocation is usually spelled out in the Agreement of Sale. Even where there are significant earnings, the seller must usually accept the fact that any allocation to "goodwill"* is going to be meager, if it is made at all. This is because the buyer must have certain depreciation benefits in order to make the acquisition feasible financially. The seller's alternative is to accept a lower price, which is generally not a very good trade-off. The seller should generally assume that virtually the entire purchase price will be allocated to fixed assets and inventory (and any accounts receivable* which might also be purchased), and not anything to goodwill* or intangible assets*.

Do not forget to include a provision in the depreciation for assets which you expect will be later acquired. What new equipment will have to be purchased? What will normal "capital expenditures"* add to depreciation? Consult management on these questions. Look especially for worn out major equipment which will have to be replaced. Sometimes owners may have let the need for replacements pile up. The same goes for building repairs which have been deferred. In addition, you should determine whether there is new technology which will have to be acquired in the future in order to keep up competitively with the rest of the industry.

If there is a reliable historic capital expenditures figure which you want to use, do not forget to increase it each year by a factor for average annual inflation. Equipment costs more and more each year.

Accurately calculating depreciation can be complicated. For example, in the third year after an acquisition, the _total_ depreciation taken might be composed of the following:
- that year's portion of the depreciation being taken on the original acquisition cost of the real estate,
- that year's portion of the depreciation being taken on the machinery and equipment originally purchased at acquisition,
- that year's portion of the depreciation being taken on the trucks and vehicles originally acquired,
- that year's portion of the depreciation being taken on machinery and equipment purchased in the second year,
- that year's portion of the depreciation being taken on machinery and equipment purchased in the third year.

All of these different depreciation accounts, one for _each_ class of assets that are acquired in _each_ year, are added up to yield the total figure.

Note that "accelerated" depreciation methods allowed by the tax laws will give a company more cash flow* in the early years, but their use entails certain disadvantages too, so consult an accountant before assuming that you will use these. Also note that you cannot use different methods of depreciation for property in the same class placed in service in the same year. A good brief treatment of depreciation can usually be found in the popular "Lasser's - Your Income Tax", which is updated annually, or any other good current tax guide. Since the tax laws change constant-

74

ly, never assume that one rule holds from year to year.

Your result at the conclusion of this step is the "Adjusted Net Operating Income".

4- Calculate Net Taxable Income.

To do this you must guess at the interest deductions which you will have. To do that you must assume a purchase price for the company, and then figure out how that price will probably be financed. You need to figure out about how much of it can be borrowed and how much will have to come from investors or from the buyer's own cash.

The amount that can be borrowed is determined by the amount of collateral the company has - its assets. In a nutshell, assume that for secured debt you can borrow as follows:

80% of the Book Value* of Accounts Receivable*
(100% if collection is guaranteed by the
buyer or seller)

80% of the Liquidation Value* of Machinery and
Equipment

65%-80% of the Market Value* of the real
estate (depending on how marketable it is)

50% of the Book Value of raw materials
inventory

0-25% of the Book Value of work-in-process
inventory, depending on the type of
materials it is composed of

85% of the Book Value of the finished goods
inventory.

These percentages are called the "advance rates".

If appraisals are available on the assets, use them. Often there is hidden value in assets because their current market value may be more than the original cost they are carried at on the books. This is particularly true with real estate, and with inventory which is accounted for using the LIFO* method (where it is assumed that the last inventory purchased is the first to be used up).

See Chapter 13 for more detailed instruction on how to determine how much can be borrowed using the assets as security.

For the purpose of calculating the anticipated interest you will be paying, try to stick with as simple a loan structure as possible. As one respected corporate finance man once said, it is very unsophisticated to try to use a sophisticated financial structure to accomplish a small deal. Rather than borrow different amounts at different rates and terms, secured by different groups of assets, try to combine your real estate and your machinery and equipment as security for one loan for a term of 10 to 15 years. Use your inventory and your accounts receivable* to secure a separate "line of credit", which will provide the money needed to actually run the business (the "working capital"*).

Otherwise, the following types of loans are common in financing an acquisition:

>Equipment Loan (a loan for a term of years, secured by the company's machinery & equipment). 5 to 7 year term, at prime interest rate plus two points.
>
>Real Estate Loan (a loan for a term of years, secured by the real estate of the company). 15 to 25 year term, at prime rate plus 1 to 2 points.
>
>Revolving Loan (or "Working Capital Loan") - A line of credit secured by inventory and accounts receivable. It has an indefinate term, and generally you can pay only the interest as long as the security for the loan remains, at prime rate plus 2 or 3 points. The principal of the loan is generally repaid only as excess profits might exist for that purpose and you feel that you want to bring your loan balance down. In other cases, the

76

loan is repaid according to some other liberal schedule set up by the lender.

Hopefully, the total amount advanced through this secured financing will be adequate to supply the entire purchase price. If not, the buyer must either sell stock in the company (equity) to investors who contribute cash to fill the gap, or take on additional debt in the form of unsecured financing. Unsecured debt is difficult to obtain. The lenders have to rely solely on your cash flow prediction for assurance that they will be repaid safely. Without any collateral to secure the debt, they will ask for higher interest rates. The investment instruments which evidence unsecured debt are generally known as "debentures". To sell them to any investor, you typically must sweeten the deal by including a privilege to convert the debt to stock, or by attaching a "warrant", which is an instrument giving its holder the right to purchase stock later at a predetermined price. Warrants can sometimes be "detached" by the debenture holder and sold to someone else. These sweeteners offset some of the risk to the investor.

Interest rates depend more upon the type of lender than upon the variety of loan. The figures here assume that the loans come from a commercial bank. For a very good treatment on the different types of lenders (commercial finance companies, insurance companies, etc.) and their expectations regarding return, see one of Nicholas Wallner's books on leveraged buyouts (Buyout Publications, Inc., San Diego, CA).

Preferred stock* is another way of raising equity, but the "interest" paid to the investor is really a dividend, and it is not deductible from income for tax purposes. Dividends are paid out of the after-tax income. Anyway, most individual purchasers prefer to finance the deal entirely with debt in order to avoid any dilution of their stock ownership.

Owner financing may be available at attractive terms, and so may government program loans. However, do not let your deal ride on the assumption that these sources of funds are going to be available to you, at least not at this stage.

Determine the total amount of interest which will be paid in each individual year for all loans. Deduct this from Operating Profit to give Taxable Net Income for each year.

If part of your plan is to use your excess cash ("cash flow safety cushion") in each year to pay off part of the principal on your revolving loan, or to retire debentures or redeem stock, then from this point on in this method, only do one year at a time. You will have to get to the end of the method for each year to see what excess cash is going to be available for this purpose. Reducing the debt or other obligations decreases the interest that will have to be paid then in the next year, thereby changing all of your calculations. The interest for that next year can not be known until the cash flow cushion for the prior year is known. Remember that you can't use <u>all</u> of the cash left at the end of each year to pay off debt - you will need to keep a pretty sizeable cash reserve on hand.

By the way, there are a number of hand-held calculators which can calculate the interest and principal payments on a loan, and they make this whole process a lot easier than if loan tables are used.

<u>NOTE:</u> Interest is an expense which is deducted on the income statement. Therefore, you want to make sure that any interest which is deducted on the adjusted historic income statement, for debts which will not exist <u>after</u> the acquisition, is added back into the operating income in each year of your projected period. Interest is usually not an "operating expense". It usually falls under "other expenses", so look for it there. Only add it back in if it is an expense which has been deducted on the way to arriving at operating profit. Note also that only the interest portion of the debt payments is included on the expense statement, not the "principal" part of those payments.

5- Determine the federal and state income tax deduct them to give you the Net Operating Income After Tax.

Use the corporate income tax rates specified under the current tax law, which changes constantly. Refer to future rates for future years if any planned rate changes have been announced. Since state income taxes are usually deductible from income for the purpose of determining federal income tax, you are usually safe in estimating the effective state tax bite at about one-half of its stated percentage rate. This saves you having to figure the state taxes first, then going back to deduct it from operating income and then calculating federal income tax based on a different amount of taxable net income. One-half is used because, at the time of this writing, the federal corporate tax rate was about 50% (46%) on taxable income over $100,000, and the value, in federal tax savings, of any deduction is generally the amount of the deduction times the tax rate which applies to you. In other words, a deductible expense of $1000 for a taxpayer in the 50% bracket will save him $500 in taxes, so that the actual cost of the expense to him is effectively only $500. You can look at your state income taxes the same way if they are deductible. So, if the state tax rate is 10% and the federal rate is 46%, then assume a combined tax bite of 51% (46% + 5%) on taxable income subject to those rates. (Different rates applying to those amounts under $100,000. See the current tax code.) Remember, these are only estimates of taxes. See you accountant for any tax figures you will be relying on.

6- Calculate the federal Investment Tax Credit which will be allowed during each year of the projection. Add that amount back in to the Net Operating Income After Tax.

Consult a current tax guide or your accountant on how to take this credit. The rules are always changing, and at the time of this writing there are proposals for eliminating the credit entirely or cutting it back severely.

The basic idea behind it, however, is that a percentage of the amount you have spent on capital improvements* and certain types of capital expenditures* is credited directly against the amount of federal income tax you owe. So, if you spend $100,000 on new machinery, and if a 10% investment tax credit applies, then the amount of tax you owe in that year is reduced by $10,000.

In addition to later capital expenditures, the credit also applies to the initial purchase of the assets of the company. There is a limit on the total amount of the credit you can take on the purchase of <u>used</u> property, and some types of property may not qualify at all. Consult your tax guide or accountant for this limit.

7- Add the Depreciation, deducted earlier, back into the Net Operating Income After Tax.

This is done because, while a deduction from taxable income for depreciation is allowed for tax purposes, it is not an expense in the sense that you actually pay out cash for it, except in the year that you actually buy the asset that you are depreciating. The IRS insists that if you have an asset that will last ten years, then you only incur a deductible expense each year to the extent of one-tenth of cost of the asset, as it wears out over that period of time. So you can only write it off to that extent each year. But, in any event, since there is no actual additional amount being paid out each year, you add the depreciation deducted back into the after-tax operating income in order to show true cash flow in those years.

8- Add back the interest expense deducted above (in step 4) to get the Net Cash Flow After Tax.

Why do we do this? Because later on in this method, after we have determined the total amount of cash flow available in each year to make loan payments, we are going to subtract those loan payments from it. And since those payments will include <u>both</u> principal and interest, you do not want to have interest subtracted twice.

9- Subtract the anticipated Capital Expenditures* in each year from Net Cash Flow After Tax.

The term "capital expenditures" refers to all amounts

which you anticipate will have to be spent in each year for new equipment, improvements to real estate, and anything else needed to keep the business running that is not written off entirely in one year as an "expense".

10- Subtract the projected annual Addition to Working Capital.*

As sales increase, so must the amount of the company's working capital*. "Working capital", for the purpose of this calculation, shall be considered to be total inventory, plus accounts receivable* and cash reserve, minus accounts payable* and other current liabilities*. In order to arrive at the total projected working capital amount needed for each year, we have to <u>separately</u> project each one of these items for <u>each</u> year.

While your accountant, from experience, may be able to quickly give you some estimates to use, if you decide to calculate working capital needed yourself, then follow these instructions:

a- <u>Inventory Projections</u>

Using your adjusted financial statement and adjusted balance sheet (see Chapter 3), calculate the "inventory turnover ratio":

   Percentage Cost of Goods Sold[2]
X Net Sales Projected for the Particular Year

= Cost of Goods Sold

---

[2] This is from the Adjusted Income Statement. Whenever anything from the income statement is prefixed with the word "percentage", it is telling you to dtermine what <u>percent</u> that item is of the amount of Net Sales in that year. In other words, take the dollar amount of that item and divide it by the dollar amount of net sales. That gives you the percentage amount of that item.

Inventory
Turnover   = $\dfrac{\text{Cost of Goods Sold}}{\text{Total Inventory at Year's End}}$
Ratio

Example: If your Adjusted Income Statement says that Cost of Goods Sold is 58.6% of Net Sales, and management tells you that, at projected Net Sales of $6,000,000, the inventory level will be about $1,500,000, then your Inventory Turnover Ratio is:

$$\dfrac{.586 \times 6{,}000{,}000}{1{,}500{,}000} = 2.344$$

Then, assume that the same ratio applies for each year of the projection, and plug your projected annual net sales figure into the formula:

$$\text{Inventory} = \dfrac{.586 \times \text{Net Sales}}{2.344}$$

Note: Before doing this, consult with the company's accountant or controller. Ask them what they think the inventory turnover ratio is, and what it should be at certain sales levels. You may wish to alter your ratio a bit in view of their comments. They may even be able to tell you from experience what the inventory level has to be at certain sales levels, thereby saving you this entire step. The same goes for the other items you are trying to calculate here. Don't be bashful in asking them to dig this information up for you.

Make sure your inventory figures include raw materials, packaging materials, work in progress, and finished goods - all at cost.

b- <u>Accounts Receivable Projections</u>

To calculate these, use your adjusted income statement and adjusted balance sheet to find the Average Collection Period (ACP) Ratio:

$$\text{ACP Ratio} = \frac{\text{Accounts Receivable}}{\dfrac{\text{Projected Sales}}{360}}$$

(Make sure you are using an accounts receivable number which corresponds to the level of sales reflected on the adjusted statement. Talk to the company's controller or accountant to make sure you are.)

Example:
$$\text{ACP Ratio} = \frac{500{,}000}{6{,}000{,}000 / 360} = 30$$

So, for each year:

$$\frac{\text{net sales}}{360} \times 30 = \text{Accnts. Rec. for that year}$$

Do this separately to project the accounts receivable for each year.

c- <u>Accounts Payable Projections</u>

First, calculate the ratio know as "Accounts Payable Days" (APD):

$$\text{APD} = \frac{\text{Accounts Payable}}{\dfrac{\text{Annual Materials Purchases}}{360}}$$

The amount of annual materials purchases should be contained in the detailed breakdown of "Cost of Goods Sold" on the income statement. Make sure the company or its accountants provide these details for you.

Example:
$$\text{APD} = \frac{\$280{,}000}{\$1{,}200{,}000 / 360} = 84$$

Second, calculate the following percentage:

$$\frac{\text{Annual Materials Purchases}}{\text{Net Sales}} = Y\%$$

Third, assuming that the same APD ratio applies in each future year, calculate accounts payable as follows:

$$\text{Accounts Payable} = \text{APD Ratio} \times \frac{Y\% \times \text{Net Sales}}{360}$$

Example:

(1) Assume ADP = 84 from example above.

(2) $Y\% = \dfrac{\$1,200,000}{6,000,000} = .20$

(3) $84 \times \dfrac{.20 \times \text{Net Sales}}{360} = \text{Accnts. Payable}$

So, if year 2 projected annual sales are $6,360,000, then:

$$84 \times \frac{.20 \times 6,360,000}{360} = \frac{\$296,000}{\text{payables for year two}}$$

d- <u>Other Current Liabilities Projections</u>

Probably the easiest way to do this is to assume that current liabilities grow each year at the same rate that net sales grow. Consult with management to make sure that the number you are starting with in year one is correct for that level of sales.

e- Cash Reserve

To determine the desireable cash reserve which the company should keep on hand at a particular level of sales, consult data published by management consulting firms such as Robert Morris Associates (Philadelphia). These firms can provide data on the average cash reserves maintained by other companies in the same industry. Many accounting firms keep this information on hand.

f- Calculate Additions to Working Capital in Each Year

(1) Plug the figures you calculated in the previous steps into the following formula:

(Accnts. Payable + Cash Reserve + Inventory)
<u>minus</u> (Accounts Payable + Other Current Liabilities)

= Total Working Capital

Do this so that you have a Total Working Capital figure for each year of the projection.

(2) Subtract the Total Working Capital figure for each year from that of the year before it. This will give you the annual <u>additions</u> to working capital.

g- <u>Subtract the Additions to Working Capital from the Net Cash Flow After Tax.</u> This will give you Cash Flow Before Debt Service.

11- Subtract Total Annual Debt Service from Cash Flow Before Debt Service:
Refer back to the work you did in Step 4. Add up the total debt payments for the entire year. The figure you use here includes both the principal and the interest portion of each payment.
On a revolving loan, remember that you are normally only paying the interest due on the principal borrowed.

The principal is not assumed to be repaid here, except to the extent that you have excess earnings available to reduce it with. In this case, you might want to make the assumption that excess earnings available at the end of each year will be used to pay back part of this debt principal. Or the earnings could be used to pay off some subordinate debt*, or non-amortizing debt*, such as debentures. However, realize that you will still want to have some sort of a cash reserve, so do not assume that all of the excess earnings will be used in this manner.

12- The amount left is your Cash Flow Safety Cushion.

Lenders demand that some reasonable safety cushion is present, and they generally demand an amount equal to 20 to 50 percent of the Cash Flow Before Debt Service. Calculate this percentage for each year.

This cushion is available for capital recovery or reinvestment. As mentioned above, you can use it to reduce the principal amount of a revolving loan, or to reduce subordinated debt, or to redeem stock. Most buyers want to reduce dilution of their stock ownership in the company, so they would use it to redeem stock held by others which was initially sold to help finance the acquisition, or to retire debentures which are convertible into stock.

Remember that after you have decided which financing obligations you want to reduce, and by how much, you must recalculate the amount of interest which will be paid in the following year, as well as the total debt service for that year. Both will be less than before.

13- Determine the present value* of the Cash Flow Cushions for each year, then add them all up.

The theory behind "present value"* is that an amount received in the future is worth less than the same amount received today. This is because you lose investment use of that money. (Inflation also decreases the value of money over time, but its effect is not taken into consideration in present value conversions.) Therefore, you are deprived of any investment income you would have earned between now and the time you actually receive it. The rate you use to determine this lessened value is known as the "discount rate". The discount rate must reflect a risk-free rate of return, plus an additional premium for the financial risk inherent in your investment in this company. Ask yourself what rate of return a typical investor would demand from an investment which is as risky as his investment in this company would be. For highly leveraged deals, the discount rate is fairly high, usually 20%-25%. For other deals, start with 15%, and then tack on an additional premium depending on the risk you perceive in the deal.

Even though these cash flow cushions are not amounts which the owners are taking out of the company when they become available, we still apply the present value concept because they are increasing the owner's equity, as well as the overall value of the business, by reducing the liabilities and outstanding stock.

Using either a calculator programmed with the present value function, or the tables contained in the Appendix, determine the present value of the Cash Flow Safety Cushion for each year, and add all these values together.

14- Determine the present value* of the assets which you expect to be present at the end of the projection period.

Traditionally, the liquidation value* of the assets is used as the basis for the present value calculation in this step. This seems to assume that the business will be terminated and the assets sold piecemeal at the end of the period. However, if you are sure that the company will be saleable as a going entity at the end of the period, then it seems reasonable to use the future anticipated <u>fair market</u> value of the assets instead of liquidation value. However, do not attribute any value to goodwill*. <u>Refer to the Glossary and to Chapter 9</u> for input on how to arrive at liquidation value or market value*.

15- Add the amount determined in Step 14 to the total amount from Step 13. Then deduct any liabilities which are expected to remain at the end of the projected period. The result is the present value of the company.

As you can see from these final steps, this valuation method can really only be properly applied to acquisitions which the purchaser plans to hold for but a limited number of years. However, by taking this analysis through Step 12, you will have prepared an excellent presentation for lenders and investors demonstrating the financial feasibility of the deal. It shows that the deal is able to safely pay for itself and meet everyone's investment return expectations.

Summary - Calculate for each year:

  Projected Net Sales (a percentage of Projected Gross Annual Sales) (Step 1)

  Operating Profit (a percentage of net sales) (Step 2)
   (plus) Depreciation amount used on the adjusted income statement (Step 3)
   (minus) Actual projected Depreciation Deduction for this year (Step 3)

= Adjusted Net Operating Income

   (minus) Interest Expense for this year (Step 4)

= Taxable Net Income

   (minus) Income Taxes (Step 5)
   (plus) Investment Tax Credit (Step 6)

= Net Operating Income After Tax

   (plus) Depreciation (Step 7)
   (plus) Interest Deducted above (Step 8)

= Net Cash Flow After Tax (Step 8)

   (minus) Projected Capital Expenditures (Step 9)
   (minus) Projected Additions to Working Capital (Step 10)

= Cash Flow Before Debt Service

   (minus) Debt Service on term loans }
   (minus) Interest on revolving loans } (Step
   (minus) Interest on unsecured debt } 11)
   (minus) Dividends on preferred stock}

= Cash Flow Safety Cushion (Step 12)
  (Then, see the text for Steps 13 to 15)

Notes:

CHAPTER 7

CAPITALIZATION OF INCOME STREAM METHOD

This method is related to the Discounted Cash Flow Method in that it looks at the flow of income as a measure of the company's value. However, this method is also related to the unfortunate (but common) use of "multiples"* - factors which are multiplied times net income in order to determine price. This practice is a shortcut of the Capitalization method. It is true that the techniques are somewhat similar in theory. Using a "multiple" of 8 times earnings is the same as dividing by a capitalization rate* of 12%. Likewise, a multiple of 10 equates with a capitalization rate of 10%.

However, for reasons which are explained more fully later on, the use of these rule-of-thumb multiples in valuation is haphazard, unprofessional, and gives unreliable results. Another problem with it is that the net income figure to which the multiple is applied is usually pulled right off the actual income statement, rather than from an adjusted income statement which more realistically reflects the financial performance of the company. For these reasons, you are urged to stick with the full procedure presented in this section. It is one of the easiest methods to use, and it is a great deal more reliable.

When To Use This Method

This method can be used anytime the business produces significant after-tax earnings, as shown by an adjusted income statement (Chapter 3).

Brief Description of the Method

This method compares the flow of income from an investment in the company to the income available from alternative forms of investment. What rate of return could you expect from other types of investments with the same level of risk? This rate of return, or "capitalization rate"*, is then applied to the net income which you believe the business will generate. The result is the value of the company from the perspective of "investment".

Typical alternative investments studied are stocks, corporate bonds, real estate investments, certificates of deposit, and government securities. Your goal is to locate investments with a level of risk similar to the risk associated with the subject company.

The major drawback of this method is that the risk inherent in most marketable securities is difficult to equate with the risk of achieving the projected earnings of a small private company. This method, therefore, involves the exercise of a significant amount of personal judgment. It is not really possible in most cases to find enough detailed earnings data on private companies to do a true comparative study. Some accountants who serve a large number of corporate clients may have sufficient data on similar companies to be able to make such a comparison, but you will probably have to settle for the data on publicly offered securities.

NOTE: In this method we compare the investor's pre-tax return from other forms of investment to the after-tax return of the company. This is appropriate to do because the after-tax earnings of the subject company will be taxed again at the personal income tax rates after they pass to the investors. This is the same as with any investment security. Corporate earnings are taxed twice - once to the corporation, and then again to the stockholders when they get their share of what is left.

See the "Summary" at the end of this chapter for a picture of the method.

Steps:

1- Prepare an Adjusted Income Statement. Refer to the Net Operating Income After-Tax on that statement.

See Chapter 3 for directions on preparing an adjusted income statement, and refer to Step 2 of Chapter 6 for additional comments.

Do not use a "pro forma*" income statement. Valuation always assumes that the company is presently operating at peak efficiency, and so the only changes which should appear on a statement used for valuation are those which are obvious and substantiated. This is your "adjusted" statement.

Unlike in the case of the Discounted Cash Flow Method, here we want net income, not net cash flow. Therefore, we do not add depreciation back into net income. Nor do we deduct anticipated capital expenditures*, additions to working capital*, or debt service*.

As you work through the preparation of your adjusted statement, bear in mind the following:

- On the income statement, interest is normally deducted as an "other expense", but the principal portion of any loan payments is not deducted and a deduction for it should therefore not be reflected on your adjusted statement. In order to estimate what the post-acquisition interest expense will be see the instructions in Step 4 of Chapter 6. Just make sure you assume a reasonable amount of debt which the new owner would incur in purchasing the company. Have the interest payments expected from that debt reflected on your adjusted statement.

93

- <u>Depreciation</u> is also usually adjusted on the income statement, because the majority of acquisitions take the form of a sale of assets, rather than a sale of stock. <u>See Step 3 of Chapter 6</u> for instructions on how to do this.

- <u>See Step 5 of Chapter 6</u> on how to calculate income taxes.

2- Do a comparative survey of the rates of return currently available on other types of investments.

Try to choose investments which have the same "term" as the period of time for which the company will probably be held by an acquirer. Assume 10 years if you don't know what this period might otherwise be. Your study might include the following types of investments:

<u>Low Risk:</u>
- government securities
- money market funds (especially with banks)
- one-year certificates of deposit at commercial banks
- municipal bonds (insured)
- treasury bills, one-year and five-year treasury bonds & notes
- zero coupon bonds
- mutual funds which invest in government or insured securities
- 10 year, industrial bonds, AAA rated
- insured municipal bond trust
- tax deferred annuity

<u>Medium Risk</u>
- uninsured municipal bond or bond unit trust
- A rated industrial bond
- mutual fund investing in income or growth type stocks
- blue-chip common stocks dividend yield
- real estate limited partnership (refer to the returns on several of the recent offerings)

- average return on the 10 or 12 most popular stock options taken by investors in the last investment cycle
- utility stocks dividend yield
- 25 year residential mortgages

High Risk:
- emerging "growth" stocks (particularly over-the-counter issues)
- oil and gas limited partnerships
- index options
- managed futures

A "typical" return for some of these investments may be hard to come by. In that case, call a stock broker and ask what the average return was from several of the more popular individual issues in the last year or last investment cycle for whatever investment it is you are inquiring about.

Then, summarize these results as follows:
Low Risk	% typical yield
Medium Risk	% typical yield
High Risk	% typical yield

Following this, decide where an investment in the subject company might lie with respect to these classifications. Remember, the general rule for investors is that "return is commensurate with risk". This means that less return should be expected from an investment in a company which is stable and uniformly profitable because it involves less risk.

An alternate approach to deciding on the appropriate rate of return is to start with what you know to be the typical rate of return investors are looking for in large 10 or 15 year commercial real estate investments, or else the return acquiring companies are generally looking for in their acquisition investments. Use this as your starting point, and then adjust the rate depending on any un-typical risk involved with this particular company or arising from the way the transaction is going to be put together. The less <u>certain</u> the predicted return on the adjusted income statement, the higher the yield required to attract the investor. Use your judgment, but justify your decisions. It would still be wise to consult current investment market returns. It also helps to talk with corporate lending officers at commercial banks to get their input on how they would view the investment and what they would expect in the way of return.

The point is to avoid using "rule-of-thumb" calculations by knowing and applying the real conditions of the current investment marketplace to this investment in an intelligent way. If you randomly assume that a return of, say, 10% would be good, then this is the same as just resorting to a "multiple" of 10. This ignores the actual returns being yielded in the current markets, and the particular risk factors inherent in the company or transaction. Such haphazard assumptions can carry you far afield. All the risk and return elements peculiar to your transaction must be recognized and accounted for.

Bear in mind that the actual purchaser of the company may have different expectations regarding rate of return.

3- Divide the Net Operating Income After-Tax (Step 1) by the Capitalization Rate selected in Step 2.

4- Reduce this figure by any liabilities which will be assumed by the purchaser. The result is the value of the company.

5- If the value arrived at in Step 4 is significantly different from the purchase price assumed in Step 1 for the purpose of estimating interest expense and depreciation, then go back and adjust those figures on the adjusted income statement to reflect a more realistic price and recalculate through Step 4.

Keep going back and forth. adjusting until the end result and the assumed price in Step 1 are fairly close. They do not have to match down to the dollar. When they get within a few thousand dollars of each other, then just interpolate.

NOTE: If this method produces a very low value for the business, this indicates that the earnings are too low to result in any goodwill* value in the company. If that is the case, then an income-based valuation method such as this one is going to produce a lower number than a method which simply looks to the value of the assets. Therefore, disregard the results of this method and instead use the Liquidation Value* of the assets as the value of the company. See Chapter 9 on liquidation value.

Summary:

$$\frac{\text{Net Operating Income Before Tax}}{\text{Capitalization Rate}}$$

(MINUS)

Assumed Liabilities

=

Value of the Company

Notes:

CHAPTER 8

EXCESS EARNINGS METHOD

When To Use This Method

This method can be used in any situation where the company produces significantly high earnings. The technique assumes that a business is worth the value of its assets, plus a premium for goodwill* if the earnings are sufficiently high. It is essentially the same as what is sometimes called the "accountant's income method", but it is probably a little easier to understand for most users.

Brief Description of the Method

This method adds together:
  1- the value of the profits earned which are in excess of the cost of financing the acquisition ("excess earnings"), and
  2- the value of the company's assets.

See the Summary at the end of this chapter for a picture of the method.

Steps:

1- Prepare an Adjusted Income Statement.
   See Chapter 3 for instructions on how to do this.
Make sure that you have made record of any changes made to the income statement so that others will

know how the statement has been adjusted.

If there has been a great deal of fluctuation in sales, obtain a stabilized figure by using a weighted average* of annual net sales for the past five years.

Here we are referring to the past income statement as an indication of how the company is probably going to perform during the next 12 months.

2- Determine the Total Market Value of all of the Tangible Operating Assets.

The "tangible operating assets" are those tangible items of property (fixed assets) which are necessary to actually run the business.

The value stated on the company's balance sheet is known as the "book value". This is not what we want. Book value is arrived at by subtracting the total depreciation (taken on the asset for tax purposes) from its original cost. Obviously, this figure may differ greatly from the actual economic value of the asset. A very valuable piece of property could have a book value of zero. What we want here is "market value": the present price at which something would change hands in an arm's length transaction between a willing buyer and a willing seller, neither being under a compulsion to act, and each having full knowledge of all relevant facts.

Asset Appraisals - The only reliable way to find the market value of specific assets is to have them professionally appraised. There are specialized firms which do nothing but appraise business assets. Do not use an appraisal which has been previously prepared for insurance purposes. First of all, there is a good chance that it is out of date. Second of all, it is probably based on "replacement value" (what it would cost to replace each of the company's assets from scratch). That is not acceptable here.

Appraisal will require physical inspection of the property, so that the condition and existence of the individual assets can be verified by the appraiser. This is one of the reasons that asset appraisals do not come cheap, but they are very important. If you are a buyer, keep in mind that an appraisal is going to have to be done eventually anyway, because your lenders are going to demand it as proof of the value of the loan collateral before they write any checks. You also want the appraisal so you can verify any estimates of value made by the seller. Do it early so that you aren't waiting until almost the date of settlement to find out what you are buying. Also, make sure that the purchase price in any agreement made prior to this is adjusted to reflect any significant differences between the estimates of value made earlier and what the appraisal shows.

Owners who are planning a sale of their company should also seriously consider having an asset appraisal done so that they know what they are selling. After all, this transaction is likely to be the owner's most important business deal ever.

Who should take the initiative on having an asset appraisal done - buyer, or seller, or lender? It might seem fair to assume that the party who initially proposed the transaction ought to pay for the appraisal. However, there is an element of judgment involved in assigning asset values, and, although the author and publisher express no opinion on this point, the suggestion is occasionally heard that the appraiser may be more apt to exercise that judgment in favor of the party who is paying the bill. A lender, for instance, prefers more conservative figures and if there was a range of possible values which the appraiser, in his professional discretion, could fairly and ethically apply to a certain asset, the lender's preference would obviously be for the lower end of this range. It seems that the mark of the professional appraiser should be his impartiality, but this is just a thought which you might want to keep in mind.

All of the following should be covered in an asset appraisal: land, buildings, inventory (raw materials, work in process, finished product, packaging materials), furnishings & fixtures, machinery & equipment, vehicles, and any other fixed assets which are necessary to run the business. Things like accounts receivable, notes receivable, and intangible assets* are not tangible operating assets and so they are not considered in this step.

Real Estate - Real estate and leasehold improvements are generally worth far more than their book value, for several reasons:

(1) Contrary to popular belief, the vast majority of realty does not rise in value right in step with the rate of inflation. This is especially the case with industrial realty. Inflation is but one factor in the real estate value. However, it generally will at least hold its original value if it is maintained in good condition and does not become functionally obsolete. This runs counter to the practice of <u>depreciating</u> real estate on the books over time.

(2) Accelerated methods of depreciation can give an even lower book value, and therefore be even more misleading in this regard.

(3) Sometimes management will "expense"* the cost of improvements to real estate, rather than adding them to the book value and then depreciating them along with the original cost of the asset. If this practice of expensing improvements has been pursued, then the added value is not reflected on the balance sheet at all.

Real estate appraisals require a different appraiser than machinery & equipment. You either want to use an "MAI" certified real estate appraiser, or average the estimates obtained from several commercial/industrial real estate brokers.

Inventory - Materials inventory which is accounted for under the LIFO* method will probably have significant hidden value. This is due to the fact that some older inventory is still being carried on the books at its original cost, yet the current market price of those materials is probably a great deal higher. These inventories should be valued instead at their current market cost. Remember that inventory is not depreciated.

Equipment - Due to inflation, equipment which is in excellent condition and not obsolete has probably depreciated very little. In this case, it is probably worth more than book value.

Tools & Dies - Tools, dies, molds, and certain other types of equipment are subject to much wear and have very short useful lives. They may also grow obsolete quickly. Their value is likely to be even less than book value.

3- Consult with management to determine the Additional Working Capital* a new owner will have to borrow in order to run the business.

Working Capital =   Current Assets, such as:
　　　　　　　　　　Inventory
　　　　　　　　　　Accounts Receivable*
　　　　　　　　　　Cash Reserve
　　　　　　　　　　(see your balance sheet for others)
　　　　　　　　- Current Liabilities*
　　　　　　　　　　(such as Accounts Payable*)

When the company is purchased, the new owner will be purchasing part of the total necessary working capital in the form of inventory and, possibly, accounts receivable. If so, the face value of those items should be deducted from the amount of working capital which the buyer would otherwise expect to have to provide in order to run the business. It is just the amount of <u>additional</u> working capital needed which we are trying to determine in this step.

On the other hand, if the purchaser will be assuming the company's current liabilities*, this <u>reduces</u> your total available working capital and increases the amount of <u>additional</u> working capital which the new owner will have to provide by the total amount of their face values.

While working capital is a combination of all those elements listed above, it is initially contributed in the form of cash. As it is spent on the business it is gradually converted into the form of labor, inventory, accounts receivable, and so on. Eventually it comes back to the form of cash (as receivables are collected) and then the cycle is repeated. Here we are just focusing on the amount of cash which the new owner will have to provide in order to keep the business rolling.

Add the figure for Additional Working Capital to the Total Asset Value determined in Step 2.

4- Determine the Cost of Financing the purchase of these assets and of borrowing the required additional working capital.

In other words, how much <u>interest</u> is the buyer going to have to pay each year when he borrows the money to buy the assets? (He will also have to borrow the extra working capital needed to run the company.) The best way to determine this is to simply contact commercial banks active in corporate lending and ask the corporate loan officer what typical interest rates are currently being charged for term loans secured by machinery & equipment and real estate, and for working capital loans secured by inventory and receivables. There are a lot of variables involved in determining the rate and terms which an individual borrower will be able to negotiate, but you can probably figure on something in the range of prime rate plus 2 to 3 points as an average lending rate.

Qualification for government sponsored industrial development financing is too difficult to predict with certainty, so counting on these lower borrowing rates at this point would be imprudent. Even so, only part of the assets would qualify for financing under most programs. You are better off just not considering them for valuation purposes.

<u>See Step 4 of Chapter 6</u> for details on determining the loan structure which you should assume for the purpose of estimating the interest costs in this step.

5- Multiply the interest rate (determined in Step 4) times the Total Asset Value (determined in Step 2) plus the Additional Working Capital needed (determined in Step 3). The result is the annual cost of financing the acquisition.

<u>NOTE:</u> If there are assets other than tangible fixed assets which will be included in the sale and paid for by the buyer (for instance, pre-paid expenses, or perhaps accounts receivable) there is some debate over whether these should be added to the total amount which will have to be financed by the buyer. As a rule, this method excludes such assets from entering into the valuation equation. This method focuses on

the value of the assets which will actually be producing income. It is an _income_ based valuation method. Some people have problems with this but that is how the method is meant to work.

6- Subtract the Cost of Financing (Step 5) from the Net Operating Income Before Tax which is shown on the adjusted income statement (Step 1). The result is the "Excess Earnings".

7- Divide the Excess Earnings by a "Capitalization Rate"* which reflects the relative risk and attractiveness which an investment in the company would have. The result is the _value_ of the excess earnings.

The capitalization rate used should correspond to the interest rate demanded of other investments with an equivilent amount of risk and an equivilent term. For example, if a deal was particularly risky, an investor might demand a return of 30% per year in exchange for their participation. For a less risky investment, they might demand a return of 15%.

Here you should note the difference between a capitalization rate and a "multiple". A multiple is a "capitalization rate*" which has been mathmatically inverted (that is, 1 is divided by the capitalization rate). However, those who use "multiples" rarely go to the trouble of formulating their multiple accurately, or of determining the proper figure to apply it to. (See the definition of "capitalization rate" in the Glossary for more on this.)

In determining the return which an investor might demand of an investment in this company consider all of the following:
- Continuity and steadiness of profits and sales over the years.
- How competitive is the market for the company's products or services? How does the company stand among that competition?
- Is the entire industry growing, declining, or stable?
- How long has the company been in operation, and how well-established is it?

- Have sales been growing rapidly, keeping pace steadily with inflation, or declining?

Note that demanding a very high rate of return is not unreasonable under certain circumstances. Most venture capital firms demand compounded annual returns of between 25% and 30%, and many leveraged buyouts have been risky enough to warrant interest rates of 20% to 25% on their secured borrowing.

Note: The value of excess earnings determined in this step is the same as what is commonly referred to as "goodwill".

8- Add the Total Asset Value (Step 2) to the Value of the Excess Earnings (Step 7). The result is the total value of the business.

Many businesses will have no Excess Earnings. In that case, the business is not regarded as being worth more than the value of its tangible assets. Attributing any significant value to trademarks, customer lists, or other intangibles is generally the same as trying to assign a value to goodwill, or excess earnings, so if the excess earnings are not there, then this is not appropriate either. In most companies, "intangibles" rarely have more than nominal value, if they have that.

If the figure calculated for Excess Earnings is a negative figure, then the assumption is that, as a "going entity", the company is not even worth the market value of its assets, and the best move for the seller in that case may be to liquidate.

Again, do not, as a rule, add the value of other assets (such as accounts receivable) which you assume the purchaser would also acquire in addition to the tangible fixed operating assets. See the "Note" in Step 5 on this point.

9- If any liabilities will be assumed by the purchaser, these must be deducted from the final value.

These include accounts payable, other accrued or current liabilities, long-term debt, accumulated unpaid stock dividends, obligations on employee benefit plans, and any other obligations. Where the ownership of the business is transferred by means of a purchase of stock, all of the company's liabilities will normally be transferred to the new owner, so their amounts must be deducted from value accordingly.

Summary:

    Total Market Value of Tangible Assets: (Step 2)
        land and building
        inventory
        equipment & machinery
        vehicles
        furnishings & fixtures

    (plus) Additional Working Capital Needed to
        run the business (Step 3)

= Total amount to be financed

    X Interest Rate (Step 4)

= Annual Cost of Financing (Step 5)

Then,
    Net Operating Income Before Tax (from adjusted
        income statement) (Step 1)

    (minus) Cost of Financing (Step 5) (above)

= Excess Earnings (Step 6)

    (divided by) Capitalization Rate (Step 7)

= Value of the Excess Earnings

    (plus) Total Value of Tangible Fixed Operating
        Assets (Step 2)
    (minus) Any liabilities of the company to be
        assumed by the buyer (Step 9)

= Total Value of the business

Alternative Approach:

A variation on this method, also commonly called the "Excess Earnings Method", is sometimes used:

Step 1 - Look at the trend in earnings (Operating Income) on the income statements for the last five years. If it is an upward trend, determine the weighted average* of the pre-tax operating income. If it is a stable or downward trend, refer only to the last year.
Add back any interest expense, and adjust the depreciation to what it would be in the future after an asset acquisition.

Step 2 - Go to the balance sheet. Look at Operating Assets (the tangible fixed assets necessary to run the business) and determine their current market value. Multiply this value times a desireable rate of return (12%, for example) which would be expected on an investment in these assets. Make sure you multiply by that percentage, not "capitalize"* by it (i.e., don't divide by the percentage).

Step 3 - Subtract the required return on assets (Step 2) from the pre-tax operating income (Step 1). The result in "Excess Earnings".

Step 4 - Divide this by a capitalization rate* which reflects the risk of the investment. (Example: 18%) This yields the "Value of the Excess Earnings".

Step 5 - Add the Value of the Excess Earnings (Step 4) to the current market value of the tangible operating assets. The result is the value of the business.

This version is really no simpler than the one originally discussed, it just differs in the way that Excess Earnings are calculated.

108

CHAPTER 9

ECONOMIC VALUE OF ASSETS METHOD

When To Use This Method

In many cases, the value of a business can not be based upon its income. Instead, its worth will be based upon the value of its assets, minus its liabilities.
This is usually the case where sales and earnings have declined steadily in recent years. In such a situation, a seller would be hard pressed to expect a premium to be paid for "goodwill"*. There are many definitions of goodwill, but for the purpose of valuing a business it is generally considered to be the value of the "excess earnings" over and above the net value of the assets. Some call it the "earnings value", and if the earnings aren't there, or if they are stagnant or in decline, then goodwill is not considered to be present.
To get a clearer picture of the concept, take a look at some of the valuation methods. One technique holds that a business is worth the value of its tangible assets, plus a premium for the earnings which are in excess of the "normal return" which would be realized by the average business holding those assets. Another holds that a business is worth the value of its assets, plus a premium for earnings in excess of the cost of financing the purchase of those assets. In either case, this premium is the goodwill. In both cases, if earnings are down, then the business is presumed to only be worth the value of the assets.

Stagnant earnings are obviously not indicative of great future potential, and goodwill will not be present in such a case.

If the Excess Earnings Method, the IRS Method, or any of the other income oriented methods indicate that goodwill value is present, then you should rely upon those techniques if they produce a higher value than this one. If those methods demonstrate that no significant earnings or goodwill value is present, then this method will probably give you the highest value for the company.

The value of intangible assets* may be included among the total asset value, but only:

1- if they would carry with them some unique advantage to an acquirer,

2- if there exists a secondary market for their sale apart from the business, and

3- if their value is separately ascertainable upon some reliable basis.

Valuing intangible assets is covered in later sections of this chapter.

Which "Measure" Of Value To Use (Market Value vs. Liquidation Value)

Assuming the other methods have shown that earnings are low enough that there is no goodwill value, and that you will therefore be looking solely to the value of the assets for the value of the company, what measure of value do we refer to in determining the value of the assets - "market value" or "liquidation value"? First consider the two approaches to selling a company's assets:

1- Sell all of the assets together so that the business can be carried on by someone else.
2- Dissolve the operation and sell the assets piecemeal, converting them into cash. This is known as liquidation, and the seller may often get more for the business by taking this route.

The first approach generally corresponds to Market Value, and the second approach generally corresponds to

110

Liquidation Value. Which approach do we take? It depends on the level of risk associated with the particular business.

Understand that a business being valued by this method has limited earnings anyway. There is automatically some pretty significant risk involved for any buyer who takes it on as an acquisition. A buyer who wants to purchase the company and continue to run it as a business needs to see two things: an apparent ability of that business to meet reasonable earnings expectations, and an ability to safely provide the payments for the large amount of debt which will generally have to be incurred in order to provide the purchase price. The buyer obviously has some changes in mind if he expects the company to be able to do this. But the farther the company now is from being able to do so, the greater the risk, and the greater the likelihood that the company will have to be valued at liquidation value.

If the company has a stagnant or downward trend in earnings, or if it shows a loss on its income statement, then it is probably best valued at liquidation value. It is going to be viewed as a "turnaround"* situation, and no buyer would have a chance of making it work out if the assets were purchased at too high a price. Note that a company can be financially stagnant, even with positive sales and earnings growth, if that growth has not been at a rate which more than keeps up with the rate of inflation.

Liquidation value is also the best approach for businesses which are relatively new, or which for other reasons do not show a history of operating success.

If the business has a realistic chance of survival after an acquisition, and if it looks like it could get through any of the foreseeable sudden disasters which might befall it, then it might be reasonable to use market value instead of liquidation value. Remember that following an acquisition the company will be carrying a large load of purchase debt, which will increase risk dramatically. If, when you assume a purchase of the company's assets at market value, the company is not able to safely carry that acquisition debt, then liquidation value is the better measure.

"Book Value"* is never really a good measure because it does not reflect the true economic value of the property being sold. Book value is based on original cost of the asset minus the depreciation taken to date.

Liquidation Value is less than market value generally. Liquidation implies a quick sale, at auction, and reflects auction prices. However, depending on how they are arranged, auctions can still be fairly competitive situations, so that the prices received can end up being quite close to market value. This is especially true for real estate and general-use types of machinery. However, for the valuator, certain loose presumptions stand with regard to liquidation value relative to market value. The following guidelines are sometimes used to estimate liquidation value in the absence of a professional appraisal:

Accounts Receivable	80-90% of Book Value
Inventory:	
Raw Materials	50-70% of Cost
Work In Progress	10-25% of Cost
Finished Goods	50% of Market Value at wholesale
Equipment & Machinery	80% of Market Value
Land & Building	65-80% of Market Value

Alternatively, the following relationships are some-

times resorted to as a rough guide:
- Replacement Cost   100%
- Market Value (used)   60%
- Liquidation Value   30-35%
- Net Book Value   20-25%

These are completely speculative, and any valuator would be justified in feeling a little nervous about using them. The results produced could be way off base in any particular case, so do not depend on them. There is no substitute for a professional asset appraisal. It is well worth the cost.

<u>Market Value</u> implies a sale negotiated at arm's length between buyer and seller, each being fully informed of all relevant facts and neither being under any compulsion to act. It does not refer to the "best" price that could be obtained. It refers to the most probable price that would be received in the market where the asset is expected to be sold. <u>See Step 2 of Chapter 8</u> for more information on determining market value. A professional asset appraisal is the only reliable way to get these figures.

Whichever measure of value is used, the valuator should be careful to exclude the value of those assets which are not necessary or relevant to the actual running of the business. And in practice, too, most buyers are firm about paying for assets which they do not want or need, so it is usually senseless to try to include them in the total asset value, even if they have no real value apart from the business.

<u>Can a business be worth less than its asset value?</u>
The premise is often heard that a business is only worth what its assets will earn. When a business is profitable and efficiently employs its assets to produce earnings, then its value is determined with reference to those earnings, instead of with reference to its assets. This is the basis for the Discounted Cash Flow Method and the Capitalization of Income Stream Method. But with poor earnings those methods can produce a very small valuation figure - one lower

113

than the value of the assets sold separately. In such a case, those results should be discarded. A business can always be liquidated, so that the liquidation value of its tangible assets is the least it would be worth, regardless of what the other methods indicate.

Remember: Don't forget to deduct from total asset value any liabilities which a buyer would have to assume in an acquisition. Also remember that in calculating the total amount that will be realized through a sale of the company's assets, you must deduct any appraisal fees, real estate brokerage commissions, auction commissions, legal fees, accounting fees, and sales tax.

Valuing Intangible Assets* - An Overview:

The most obvious intangible asset is goodwill*, discussed above and in the chapter on the Excess Earnings Method. There are often many other intangible assets associated with the typical business, but that does not necessarily mean they have an ascertainable value. Valuing intangibles is one of the most difficult aspects of determining business worth.

In general, the result of the income-oriented valuation methods automatically include the value of goodwill and other intangible assets. There are situations, however, during the course of negotiation, when the value of an intangible asset attached to an ongoing business becomes an issue. In addition, when a company's value is determined solely by the value of its assets, the value of an intangible will occasionally be included in the tally. These instances are:

(1) When all of the assets of the company are being sold together so that the business can still be carried on by someone else. However, in order to warrant additional value, the intangible must provide a specific and unique advantage of some kind to the new owner. Even so, it is difficult to convince a buyer to pay additional for such intangibles. In practice, whatever value they do have usually must be thrown into the deal by the seller as an extra for the buyer who is willing the purchase all of the tangible assets as a

whole. It is much more convenient and much less costly for a seller to sell all of the assets as a lot than it is to dispose of them piecemeal, so it is generally worth it to forget about trying to demand additional payment for any intangibles in such a case. Besides, their value is likely to be nominal anyway, and with the valuation of intangibles as difficult as it is, it is well worth not having to go through that process.
However, the case for the seller getting paid something extra is bolstered when an intangible has a recognized, secondary market for its sale apart from the business.

(2) When the business is being liquidated, and the intangible asset can be sold apart from the business in a reliable secondary market that exists for it.

In most acquisitions, attributing value to intangible assets is usually just a substitute for attributing value to goodwill or excess earnings. Intangibles such as brandnames and customer lists are things which help make a collection of assets a "business", so the value connected with them is often thought of as an "ongoing business value" that is necessarily included in the company. However, this is also essentially the same as goodwill. If the other methods indicate that there is no goodwill or earnings value in the business over and above the value of the assets, then attempting to attribute value separately to intangibles is not appropriate. Only where there exists a secondary market for that particular type of intangible asset, so that it can be readily sold as a separate matter, can an intangible be said to have value when there is otherwise no goodwill value present in the earnings of the company. An example might be the case of a liquor license. However, most intangibles have no value when separated from the company.

Remember that the seller is sometimes quite unrealistic about the value of a particular asset or intangible. Things like secret processes or customized equipment may perform special functions, but that does not mean that anyone wants or needs those functions performed.

Note On Economic Life of an Intangible Asset

In the methods that follow, it is generally necessary to estimate the "economic life" of the intangible asset being valued. This refers to the period of time for which the intangible will bring an economic benefit to its owner. However, it must be remembered that the intangible may have a realistic economic life which is much shorter than its legal life. A patent, for instance, may be legally valid for a certain number of years, but it will probably only result in a financial advantage to its holder for a few of those years before product demand diminishes or it becomes outmoded by even better products.

Also keep in mind that the advantage gained from an intangible <u>gradually</u> diminishes over time. It usually does not just stop all at once. There will probably be less economic benefit in the later years than in the beginning. You should reflect this gradual reduction in your calculations.

Methods of Valuing Intangible Assets

1- <u>Pricing Advantage (or Profit Contribution)</u>

In this case you determine the additional net income which the intangible asset brings to the business over similar businesses not benefited by this intangible. An example might be a brand name with a high recognition level among consumers.
Steps:
(1) Determine the additional amount of price that can be charged by the company for each unit of the product sold, over the price charged by competing products not benefited by the intangible. Use wholesale price to distributors, not retail price, unless

the manufacturer is also the retailer.

(2) Multiply that price advantage times the number of units sold annually. Use the volume sold in the current year.

(3) Determine the number of years that the intangible will probably continue to benefit the owner in this way - the "economic life".

(4) Calculate the present value* of this additional amount which will be received in each year. Use a discount rate equal to the annual return an investor would expect on a medium risk investment made for the same number of years. Deduct any special costs associated with maintaining this intangible.

(5) Total the present values for all these years. The result is the value of the intangible.

This method is best for items which have a determinable life, such as a patent or copyright. Remember that the realistic economic useful life of a patent, copyright, licensing agreement, etc. may be much shorter that its legal life.

Some specific uses:
- Brand names and registered trademarks
- Copyrights
- Patents - Remember that new competitive technology normally diminishes the value of patent protection well before the legal life of the patent has expired, so be realistic and study competing technology before making your decision.
- Unpatented special processes - Use a high-risk capitalization rate for determining present value, and use one-half to one-third the expected economic life of a similar <u>patented</u> process. This is done in order to reflect the greater risk resulting from the lack of patent protection.
- Customer Lists - Use the following special approach:

(1) Determine the annual sales contribution made by each individual repeat customer on the list. Add these up. Determine the resulting net profit after tax. (Do this by using the percentage figure for Net Profit After Tax on the company's last full income

117

statement.)

(2) Determine the useful life of the list by dividing 100% by the average annual percentage of turnover on the list (lost customers). For example, a 10% annual turnover means a useful life of 10 years.

(3) Assume that the net profit determined in Step 1 will continue for the number of years determined in Step 2. However, diminish the net profit contribution for each succeeding year from that of the year before it by the same percentage used in Step 2 to describe the rate of turnover. In other words, if the turnover rate is 10%, then the first year will be 100% of the total possible profit contribution by customers on the list, and the second year will be 90%, the third year 80%, and so on for 10 years.

(4) Bring the profit contribution from each year into present value* using a high risk capitalization rate. Add up the present values.

2- Royalty and Licensing Agreements

Steps:
(1) Determine the realistic economic life of the agreement.
(2) Project the sales of the item for each year of that period.
(3) Apply the royalty rate to that sales figure for each year.
(4) Deduct any special expenses associated with the licence or agreement, including special accounting or audit costs.
(5) Bring the result for each year into present value*.
(6) Add up the present values from each year.

This method can be used to value unlicensed brand names or trademarks, but it requires a great deal of speculation on the probable royalty percentage which could be received, on the length of economic life, and on the number of units which might be sold under the license. Determining that it could be successfully licensed at all is extremely speculative in itself. Overall, there are generally too many unpredictable factors to permit this.

3- <u>Profit Contribution By Cost Savings</u>

Use this method when the intangible provides the company with a unique cost savings which is not enjoyed by its competition.

Steps:

(1) Determine the additional amount of cost a competitor lacking this advantage has to pay in order to produce the same number of units which the subject company produces annually.

(2) Determine the realistic life of this advantage before it expires or before the competition is likely to catch up.

(3) Determine the present value* of the cost savings for each year. Use a discount rate equal to an investor's expected rate of return on a medium risk investment of the same duration. (For example, 15% for 6 years.)

(4) Add up the present values for each year.

Some specific uses:

- Contracts for the purchase of materials at advantageous prices. Bring each year's cost advantage into present value.

- Covenants Not To Compete (Contractual promises by competitors, or potential competitors, not to compete with the company in certain areas of business, lasting for a specified period of years.) Specific directions:

(1) Compute lost sales which would occur with certainty if the competing business were allowed to exist. Do this for each year of the economic life of the agreement. Remember that as the new owner of an acquired business gradually builds up his own business goodwill, the value of the covenant not to compete will diminish in value, so the potential "lost sales" projected should decline each year.

(2) For each year, determine the amount of lost Net Income After Tax which corresponds to the amount of potential lost sales for that year.

(3) Bring the amount of potential lost Net

Income from each year into present value. Use a high risk capitalization rate.
(4) Add the present values together.

More Specific Uses:
- Patented Processes - Use a medium risk capitalization rate in determining present value.
- <u>Un</u>patented Special Processes - To reflect the greater risk due to a lack of patent protection, use a high risk capitalization rate, and one-half to one-third of the realistic economic life of a similar patented process.
- Tax Loss Carryforwards - (An accumulation of losses written off by the company, for which there have not been sufficient taxable earnings to be offset by them. They can be used by the corporation to offset taxable income in future years - "carried forward".) Consult your accountant. There are important restrictions in the use of the tax loss carryforward which you must be advised of. Your accountant can also estimate the anticipated tax savings which they would bring if usable. Bring the tax savings predicted for each year into present value using a high risk capitalization rate, because the company has obviously had some problems which led to the loss, and because of the risk the IRS will disallow the use of the carryforward on audit.

4- <u>Cost To Create An Intangible Asset</u>

Refer to the original cost to create the intangible. Be careful, because cost is not usually indicative of true value. It generally overstates it, so your figure will probably have to be scaled back, perhaps significantly. Tremendous costs may have been incurred in the creation of an intangible which actually brings no real traceable income advantage to the company. If this is the case, then no matter how much was spent, no value can be attributed to it. This is the case with many patents.
Some specific uses:
- Copyrights
- Specialized mailing lists - (For useful life,

use 100% divided by annual turnover rate)
- Patented processes developed through extensive research
- Patents applied for - (Research & development work done for a yet ungranted patent)
- Customer lists

5- <u>Cost to Purchase the Intangible Asset</u>

Used only for intangibles which have an active secondary market for their resale - such as:
- Franchise agreements - Reduce the anticipated value to reflect any transferability or buy-back restrictions in the agreement.
- Transferable licenses - (Liquor license, etc.)

6- <u>Contracts Which Provide Income (Sales Contracts)</u>
Bring the Net Income After Tax which is expected for each future year of the contract into present value and add up.

7- <u>Employment Contracts</u>

Calculate the cost which would be incurred by the company in replacing the individual. Generally, include the costs of training new personnel only to the point where they would become as effective as the subject employee in carrying out the specific duties which the employment contract was intended to protect and reserve for the company. Value only the <u>additional</u> costs <u>over and above</u> those of maintaining the individual covered by the contract.

For example, consider the case of a person under contract who is important to the company because of her marketing ability. If only 50% of her time is normally spent on marketing and the rest is spent on general management, the company would probably have to hire two people to effectively replace her - a marketing person and a general manager. So,

(1) Add the costs of the two anticipated salaries.
(2) Deduct the salary amount which is paid to the covered individual.
(3) Deduct a portion of each of the replacement

salaries to the extent that these parties would be able to provide increased or additional services to the company over and above what the subject employee does.

(4) Assume that the additional cost will be incurred in each remaining year of the contract term. Bring the amount for each year into present value using a medium risk discount rate.

(5) Add up the present values.

(6) Add any costs which would be associated with replacing the individual, such as recruiter's fees, training seminars, and so on.

You may discover that, after deducting that part of the replacements' salaries which reflect their additional contributions to the firm (Step 3), that there is no additional cost at all, other than hiring costs.

In the case where only one person is hired to replace the covered individual, what is valued is the cost of training and maintaining this person only to the point where he is as effective as the covered person at his duties, assuming they are paid the same salary. For instance, if it would take six months for the replacement to come up to par with the covered employee, then the cost to the company is only the present value of a half-year's salary, plus hiring costs and additional training costs, minus the gradually increasing value of the new employee's contribution to the company during that period. If the new person has to be paid a higher salary to boot, then the difference between the two salaries incurred during the remaining contract term would also be included.

Remember: Read any type of contract carefully. It may reveal exposure to a liability which actually detracts from the overall value of the business. It also may obligate the new owner to something which is considered a detriment rather than an advantage, therefore affecting value negatively. Always consult an attorney with regard to any legal document.

CHAPTER 10

NET WORTH PER BOOKS APPROACH

The Concept of "Net Worth" and Its Place In Valuation

Net Worth Per Books is not really a valuation method, but the concept is occasionally used during negotiation of the purchase price of a business, or as a point of reference for comparing deals.

The suggestion of a purchase price at Book Value or Net Worth[1] is often employed as a bargaining position when a buyer wants to purchase a company cheaply which should be valued at asset value. In other words, when there is no real "goodwill" or earnings value in the company, and its value is therefore determined solely with reference to the economic value of its assets, Book Value is one commonly used way of referring to that total asset value. For more information on when the economic value of the assets is used as the basis for valuing a company, see Chapter 9. This section is really just supplementary to that one.

The problem with Net Worth or Book Value is that it does not accurately reflect the true economic value of the assets being sold in most cases. For that reason, it is not something which should be relied upon (like

---

[1]Note: In this chapter "net worth" and "book value" of the company are used synonymously. Technically, they are different, as explained later on.

123

market or liquidation value) in determining true worth.

Definition of Net Worth (or Book Value)

Net Worth is the difference between the Total Assets and the Total Liabilities, as shown on the company's balance sheet. It is also referred to as "Owner's Equity", because it is the worth of the business to its owners in terms of balance sheet values. The term "Book Value" is often used as slang for Net Worth, but "book value" technically refers to that value which an individual asset is carried at on the balance sheet. It is equal to its original cost minus all depreciation taken on it to date. On the balance sheet, assets are usually grouped together according to category - machinery & equipment, tools & dies, data processing equipment, and so on. The figure shown on the balance sheet for each category is the total of the book values for all the assets in that category.

Although the terms are used somewhat interchangeably in this chapter, a purchase price at "Net Worth" would indicate an arrangement where the buyer takes on the existing liabilities of the company, as is the case where the transaction takes the form of a purchase of stock. A purchase price at "Book Value" would generally be presumed to refer to the total of the book values of all the assets of the company, without assuming any liabilities.

When the Net Worth Approach Is Used

Net Worth should never be used as the sole determinant of purchase price, but there are circumstances where it is commonly used as a reference point for negotiation. In such cases, the company's worth is really being based on asset value, and Net Worth is simply being used as another approach to setting the

There it is said that, as a general rule, the buyer wants to purchase the company at, or close to, book value. This, however, is just one way of trying to end up with a purchase price which is below market value and liquidation value, and which can therefore probably be financed completely with secured loans. (By the way, in this situation, any intangible assets* which can not be used as collateral for the secured loans are usually excluded from the total computation. These might include goodwill (of course), capitalized research and development expenditures, patents, processes, and so on.)

In addition, a company's Book Value often becomes psychologically relevant as a strategic matter in price negotiation. Where a large parent corporation is divesting a certain subsidiary or operating unit, it generally wants a price which at least covers its remaining investment in that business. In other words, it wants to get its money out of it, to the extent that it has not yet been written off. This is generally the Book Value of the company according to its balance sheet. The parent will usually insist upon a price which at least allows it to break even in this way. And if the business has not been performing all that nicely, such a seller often will not insist on a price that is much higher than book. Therefore, the buyer generally knows that his price has to at least come up to book value unless the business is really in bad shape and the parent is desperate to unload it. Still, it usually proves to be an embarrassment for someone in the parent's organization when a company is sold for below book value, particularly the person who insisted upon the original acquisition of it in the first place, so book value can be anticipated as the bottom line in most cases where the business is not patently unsound. On the other hand, a buyer looking at a company which has performed poorly knows, in most cases, that he will not have to offer much more than book value to purchase the unit. Depending on how poorly it has done, he may even get a price below book value. The business could be hemorrhaging and causing uncomfortable losses for the parent, who has neither the interest nor the inclination to try to turn it around.

the parent, who has neither the interest nor the inclination to try to turn it around.

There may be times when book value is greater than the economic value of the assets. In that case, book value obviously overstates the worth of the business and true economic value of the assets is the only fair approach. See Chapter 9 for how to determine asset value of a business.

There may be cases where Net Worth or Book Value is very close to economic value. One is where the business is relatively new. Another is where a large proportion of the company's tangible assets are regularly replaced. But never assume that book value is the same as economic value. Always assess economic value as a separate matter.

Why Net Worth Is Not A Reliable Measure Of Value

The individual book values that Net Worth is based on are usually misleading as a measure of value. The book value for each asset is a product of the accounting methods used and it has nothing to do with true value to the average buyer out in the market place for such assets. This is because the depreciation subtracted annually generally does not equal the actual incremental loss of value in the assets due to time and wear. This departure from reality is accentuated when "accelerated" methods of depreciation have been used by the company in order to speed up the write-off of these assets.

In addition, certain assets hold their value much better than others and actually depreciate very little in value over time. In fact, they may even rise in value, due to inflation, if they are maintained in excellent condition. Real estate is the classic example of this. The point is that traditional accounting methods do not produce balance sheet values which reflect true economic worth. Yet, despite this fact, businessmen will often rely on book value or net worth as an indication of true value. It is recommended that use of the Net Worth concept be limited to those price negotiation situations discussed earlier in the chapter.

CHAPTER 11

THE INTERNAL REVENUE SERVICE METHOD

When To Use This Method

The Internal Revenue Service has its own approach to the valuation of a business. The IRS method usually comes into play when gift or estate taxes are being assessed or disputed. Understanding the IRS viewpoint is essential to being able to work successfully to resolve such questions. Besides, an erroneous valuation can cost the estate considerable tax dollars. A well prepared and thoroughly documented valuation report based on other methods will often be accepted by the service as indicative of value, although its weight in resolving the issue would obviously be strengthened considerably if the IRS method is included in it as well.

The IRS approach is likely to be deferred to when any taxation dispute arises: allocation of purchase price, depreciation deductions, recapture of tax benefits, and so on. Whenever the valuation is to be used for tax purposes, it would be wise to include the IRS method in your study. And always consult your accountant when tax matters are involved.

Brief Description of the Method

The Treasury Department first promulgated its valuation formula with ARM 34 and 68 (Appeal and Review Memorandums). Since then, its policy has been more clearly set forth in a series of Revenue Rulings and Revenue Procedures. These have been reproduced later in this section.

ARM 34 and 68 - Discusses the formula for valuing goodwill (quoted in Rev. Rul. 65-192).

Rev. Rul. 65-192 - "The general approach, methods and factors outlined in Revenue Ruling 59-60,... are equally applicable for income and other tax purposes."

Rev. Rul. 59-60 - Its purpose is "to outline and review in general the approach, methods, and factors to be considered in valuing the shares of the capital stock of closely held corporations for estate and gift tax purposes."

Rev. Procedure 66-49 - Deals with how to report how valuations are arrived at to the Internal Revenue Service.

Rev. Rul. 68-609 - Discusses return on tangible assets and capitalization rates for intangibles, when the IRS income approach is used. (Clarifies and expands on ARM 34.)

Rev. Procedure 77-12 - Describes the method for allocating a lump sum purchase price to inventories.

Always read the entire ruling, research more recent developments, and consult your accountant or tax attorney. Tax rules change constantly.

The IRS method of determining the value of a business adds the value of the Net Tangible Assets to the capitalized value of the Excess Earnings (goodwill). Most estate tax issues involving the IRS approach center on the value of goodwill*.

Steps (Summarized):

1- Using the balance sheets for the last five years, determine the average value of the Net Tangible Assets during that period. (Net Tangible Assets = Total Assets - Identifiable Intangible Assets - Liabilities). Averages may be weighted to consider trends.

2- Determine the company's Return on the Net Tangible Assets by multiplying the figure from Step 1 by 8 to 10 percent (or use a rate which corresponds to the normal rate of return on assets within the particular industry). Use a lower rate for a business associated with a lower risk factor.

3- Determine the average Net Profit Before-Tax from the last five years.

4- Subtract the figure from Step 3 from the figure from Step 2. The result is the company's Excess Earnings (i.e., earnings in excess of what a "typical company" would have produced from those tangible assets).

5- Capitalize* the Excess Earnings from Step 4 at a rate between 15 and 20 percent. (In other words, divide Excess Earnings by .15 to .20). The result is the value of the "Goodwill" of the business. (This may also be thought of as the value of the intangible assets.) Use a lower capitalization rate for a business associated with lower risk.

6- Add the result in Step 5 to the value of the Net Tangible Assets determined in Step 1. The result is the value of the business.

This is just a summary of the usual procedure. See the actual Revenue Rulings and Revenue Procedures for a full treatment of the method.

Special Considerations in Estate Tax Valuations

Note that if the business was run primarily by its owner, it is usually going to be worth less with that person no longer on the scene. It is quite possible that this person was largely responsible for the success of the company. The loss is much more significant than it would have been had the company been "professionally managed" (i.e., greater division of authority and more broadly developed management structures). Therefore, the absence of this party is definitely going to have a detrimental effect on business and justify a lower valuation.

In addition, while valuations conducted as preparation for the sale of a company inevitably have some element of anticipation of future profits in them, those done for estate tax purposes never should. Valuation should never be based upon conjecture concerning what has not yet occurred. Yet, in some ways they are still future oriented - for instance, in the selection of capitalization rates used to reduce future earnings to present value, in the adjustment of historical income statements to show how expenses might look under different ownership and management, and so on. However, a valuation for estate tax purposes should be based entirely on a summary of the company's present situation, as indicated by its most recent past, and not on expectations of different results for the future. Make sure that what is being valued is "what is", and not "what will be".

Once again, remember that all transactions have important tax consequences. Always consult your accountant and have your valuation study reviewed prior to making any decisions in dependence upon it.

The Internal Revenue Service Rules (Reproduced)

26 CFR 1.1001-1: Computation of gain or loss.   Rev. Rul. 65-192

> The general approach, methods and factors outlined in Revenue Ruling 59-60, C.B. 1959-1, 237, for use in valuing closely-held corporate stocks for estate and gift tax purposes are equally applicable to valuations thereof for income and other tax purposes and also in determinations of the fair market values of business interests of any type and of intangible assets for all tax purposes.
>
> The formula approach set forth in A.R.M. 34, C.B. 2, 31 (1920), and A.R.M. 68, C.B. 3, 43 (1920), has no valid application in determinations of the fair market values of corporate stocks or of business interests, unless it is necessary to value the intangible assets of the corporation or the intangible assets included in the business interest. The formula approach may be used in determining the fair market values of intangible assets only if there is no better basis therefor available. In applying the formula, the average earnings period and the capitalization rates are dependent upon the facts and circumstances pertinent thereto in such case.

SECTION 1. PURPOSE.

The purpose of this Revenue Ruling is to furnish information and guidance as to the usage to be made of suggested methods for determining the value as of March 1, 1913, or of any other date, of intangible assets and to identify those areas where a valuation formula set forth in A.R.M. 34, C.B. 2, 31 (1920), as modified by A.R.M. 68, C.B. 3, 43 (1920), both quoted in full below should and should not be applied. Since it appears that such formula has been applied to many valuation issues for which it was never intended, the Internal Revenue Service reindicates its limited application.

SEC. 2. BACKGROUND.

A.R.M. 34 was issued in 1920 for the purpose of providing suggested formulas for determining the amount of March 1, 1913, intangible asset value lost by breweries and other businesses connected with the distilling industry, as a result of the passage of the 18th Amendment to the Constitution of the United States. A.R.M. 68 was issued later in the same year and contained a minor revision of the original ruling so that its third formula would be applied in accordance with its purpose and intent.

SEC. 3. STATEMENT OF POSITION.

.01 Although the formulas and approach contained in A.R.M. 34, were specifically aimed at the valuation of intangible assets of distilling and related companies as of March 1, 1913, the last two paragraphs of the ruling seemingly broaden it to make its third formula applicable to almost any kind of enterprise. The final sentences, however, limit the purpose of such formula by stating that "In * * * all of the cases the effort should be to determine what net earnings a purchaser of a business on March 1, 1913, might reasonably have expected to receive from it, * * *, "and by providing certain checks and alternatives. Also, both A.R.M. 34 and A.R.M. 68 expressly stated that such formula was merely a rule for guidance and not controlling in the presence of "better evidence" in determining the value of intangible assets. Furthermore, T.B.R. 57, C.B. 1, 40 (1919), relating to the meaning of "fair market value" of property received in exchange for other property, which was published before A.R.M. 34 and A.R.M. 68 and has not been revoked, set forth general principles of valuation that are consistent with Revenue Ruling 59-60, C.B. 1959-1, 237. Moreover, in S.M. 1609, C.B. III-1, 48 (1924) it was stated that "The method suggested in A.R.M. 34 for determining the value of intangibles is * * * controlling only in the absence of better evidence." As said in *North American Service Co., Inc.* v. *Commissioner*, 33 T.C. 677, 694' (1960), acquiescence, C.B. 1960-2, 6, "an A.R.M. 34 computation would not be conclusive of the existence and value of good will if better evidence were available * * *."

.02 Revenue Ruling 59-60 sets forth the proper approach to use in the valuation of closely-held corporate stocks for estate and gift tax purposes. That ruling contains the statement that no formula can be devised that will be generally applicable to the multitude of different valuation issues. It also contains a discussion of intangible value in closely-held corporations and some of the elements which may support such value in a given business.

SEC. 4. DELINEATION OF AREAS IN WHICH SUGGESTED METHODS WILL BE EFFECTIVE.

.01 The general approach, methods, and factors outlined in Revenue Ruling 59-60 are equally applicable to valuations of corporate stocks for income and other tax purposes as well as for estate and gift tax purposes. They apply also to problems involving the determination of the fair market value of business interests of any type, including partnerships, proprietorships, etc., and of intangible assets for all tax purposes.

.02 Valuation, especially where earning power is an important factor, is in essence a process requiring the exercise of informed judgment and common sense. Thus, the suggested formula approach set forth in A.R.M. 34, has no valid application in determinations of the fair market value of corporate stocks or of business interests unless it is necessary to value the intangible assets of the corporation or the intangible assets included in the business interest. The formula approach may be used in determining the fair market values of intangible assets only if there is no better basis therefor available. In applying the formula, the average earnings period and the capitalization rates are dependent upon the facts and circumstances pertinent thereto in each case. See *John Q. Shunk et al.* v. *Commissioner*, 10 T.C. 293, 304-5 (1948), acquiescence, C.B. 1948-1, 3, affirmed 173 Fed. (2d) 747 (1949); *Ushco Manufacturing Co., Inc.* v. *Commissioner*, Tax Court Memorandum Opinion entered March 10, 1945, affirmed 175 Fed. (2d) 821 (1945); and *White & Wells Co.* v. *Commissioner*, 19 B.T.A. 416, nonacquiescence C.B. IX-2, 87 (1930), reversed and remanded 50 Fed. (2d) 120 (1931).

SEC. 5. QUOTATION OF A.R.M. 34.

For convenience, A.R.M. 34 reads as follows:

The Committee has considered the question of providing some practical formula for determining value as of March 1, 1913, or of any other date, which might be considered as applying to intangible assets, but finds itself unable to lay down any specific rule of guidance for determing the value of intangibles which would be applicable in all cases and under all circumstances. Where there is no established market to serve as a guide the question of value, even of tangible assets, is one largely of judgment and opinion, and the same thing is even more true of intangible assets such as good will, trade-marks, trade brands, etc. However, there are several methods of reaching a conclusion as to the value of intangibles which the Committee suggests may be utilized broadly in passing upon questions of valuation, not to be regarded as controlling, however, if better evidence is presented in any specific case.

Where deduction is claimed for obsolescence or loss of good will or trade-marks, the burden of proof is primarily upon the taxpayer to show the value of such good will or trade-marks on March 1, 1913. Of course, if good will or trademarks have been acquired for cash or other valuable considerations subsequent to March 1, 1913, the measure of loss will be determined by the amount of cash or value of other considerations paid therefor, and no deduction will be allowed for the value of good will or trade-marks built up by the taxpayer since March 1, 1913. The following suggestions are made, therefore, merely as suggestions for checks upon the soundness and validity of the taxpayers' claims. No obsolescence or loss with respect to good will should be allowed except in cases of actual disposition of the asset or abandonment of the business.

In the first place, it is recognized that in numerous instances it has been the practice of distillers and wholesale liquor dealers to put out under well-known and popular brands only so much goods as could be marketed without affecting the established market price therefor and to sell other goods of the same identical manufacture, age, and character under other brands, or under no brand at all, at figures very much below those which the well-known brands commanded. In such cases the difference between the price at which whisky was sold under a given brand name and also under another brand name, or under no brand name, multiplied by the number of units sold during a given year gives an accurate determination of the amount of profit attributable to that brand during that year, and where this practice is continued for a long enough period to show that this amount was fairly constant and regular and might be expected to yield annually that average profit, by capitalizing this earning at the rate, say, of 20 per cent, the value of the brand is fairly well established.

Another method is to compare the volume of business done under the trademark or brand under consideration and profits made, or by the business whose good will is under consideration, with the similar volume of business and profit made in other cases where good will or trade-marks have been actually sold for cash, recognizing as the value of the first the same proportion of the selling price of the second, as the profits of the first attributable to brands or good will, is of the similar profits of the second.

The third method and possibly the one which will most frequently have to be applied as a check in the absence of data necessary for the application of the preceding ones, is to allow out of average earnings over a period of years prior to March 1, 1913, preferably not less than five years, a return of 10 per cent upon the average tangible assets for the period. The surplus earnings will then be the average amount available for return upon the value of the intangible assets, and it is the opinion of the Committee that this return should be capitalized upon the basis of not more than five years' purchase—that is to say, five times the amount available as return from intangibles should be the value of the intangibles.

In view of the hazards of the business, the changes in popular tastes, and the difficulties in preventing imitation or counterfeiting of popular brands affecting the sales of the genuine goods, the Committee is of the opinion that the figure given of 20 per cent return on intangibles is not unreasonable, and it recommends that no higher figure than that be attached in any case to intangibles without a very clear and adequate showing that the value of the intangibles was in fact greater than would be reached by applying this formula.

The foregoing is intended to apply particularly to businesses put out of existence by the prohibition law, but will be equally applicable so far as the third formula is concerned, to other businesses of a more or less hazardous nature. In the case, however, of valuation of good will of a business which consists of the manufacture or sale of standard articles of every-day necessity not subject to violent fluctuations and where the hazard is not so great, the Committee is of the opinion that the figure for determination of the return on tangible assets might be reduced from 10 to 8 or 9 per cent, and that the percentage for capitalization of the return upon intangibles might be reduced from 20 to 15 per cent.

In any or all of the cases the effort should be to determine what net earnings a purchaser of a business on March 1, 1913, might reasonably have expected to receive from it, and therefore a representative period should be used for averaging actual earnings, eliminating any year in which there were extraordinary factors affecting earnings either way. Also, in the case of the sale of good will of a going business the percentage rate of capitalization of earnings applicable to good will shown by the amount actually paid for the business should be used as a check against the determination of good will value as of March 1, 1913, and if the good will is sold upon the basis of capitalization of earnings less than the figures above indicated as the ones ordinarily to be adopted, the same percentage should be used in figuring value as of March 1, 1913.

Sec. 6. Quotation of A.R.M. 68.

Also for convenience, A.R.M. 68 reads as follows:

The Committee is in receipt of a request for advice as to whether under A.R.M. 34 the 10 per cent upon tangible assets is to be applied only to the net tangible assets or to all tangible assets on the books of the corporation, regardless of any outstanding obligations.

The Committee, in the memorandum in question, undertook to lay down a rule for guidance in the absence of better evidence in determining the value as of March 1, 1913, of good will, and held that in determining such value, income over an average period in excess of an amount sufficient to return 10 per cent upon tangible assets should be capitalized at 20 per cent. Manifestly, since the effort is to determine the value of the good will, and therefore the true net worth of the taxpayer as of March 1, 1913, the 10 per cent should be applied only to the tangible assets entering into net worth, including accounts and bills receivable in excess of accounts and bills payable.

In other words, the purpose and intent are to provide for a return to the taxpayer of 10 per cent upon so much of his investment as is represented by tangible assets and to capitalize the excess of earnings over the amount necessary to provide such return, at 20 per cent.

SEC. 7. EFFECT ON OTHER DOCUMENTS.

Although the limited application of A.R.M. 34 and A.R.M. 68 is reindicated in this Revenue Ruling, the principles enunciated in those rulings are not thereby affected.

Valuation of intangible assets of a business where separate appraisal of tangible and intangible assets may not be possible. See Rev. Rul. 65-193, page 370.

26 CFR 20.2031-2: Valuation of stocks and bonds.   Rev. Rul. 59-60
(Also Section 2512.)
(Also Part II, Sections 811 (k), 1005, Regulations 105, Section 81.10.)

> In valuing the stock of closely held corporations, or the stock of corporations where market quotations are not available, all other available financial data, as well as all relevant factors affecting the fair market value must be considered for estate tax and gift tax purposes. No general formula may be given that is applicable to the many different valuation situations arising in the valuation of such stock. However, the general approach, methods, and factors which must be considered in valuing such securities are outlined.
> Revenue Ruling 54-77, C.B. 1954-1, 187, superseded.

SECTION 1. PURPOSE.

The purpose of this Revenue Ruling is to outline and review in general the approach, methods and factors to be considered in valuing shares of the capital stock of closely held corporations for estate tax and gift tax purposes. The methods discussed herein will apply likewise to the valuation of corporate stocks on which market quotations are either unavailable or are of such scarcity that they do not reflect the fair market value.

SEC. 2. BACKGROUND AND DEFINITIONS.

.01 All valuations must be made in accordance with the applicable provisions of the Internal Revenue Code of 1954 and the Federal Estate Tax and Gift Tax Regulations. Sections 2031(a), 2032 and 2512(a) of the 1954 Code (sections 811 and 1005 of the 1939 Code) require that the property to be included in the gross estate, or made the subject of a gift, shall be taxed on the basis of the value of the property at the time of death of the decedent, the alternate date if so elected, or the date of gift.

.02 Section 20.2031-1(b) of the Estate Tax Regulations (section 81.10 of the Estate Tax Regulations 105) and section 25.2512-1 of the Gift Tax Regulations (section 86.19 of Gift Tax Regulations 108) define fair market value, in effect, as the price at which the property would change hands between a willing buyer and a willing seller when the former is not under any compulsion to buy and the latter is not under any compulsion to sell, both parties having reasonable knowledge of relevant facts. Court decisions frequently state in addition that the hypothetical buyer and seller are assumed to be able, as well as willing, to trade and to be well informed about the property and concerning the market for such property.

.03 Closely held corporations are those corporations the shares of which are owned by a relatively limited number of stockholders. Often the entire stock issue is held by one family. The result of this situation is that little, if any, trading in the shares takes place. There is, therefore, no established market for the stock and such sales as occur at irregular intervals seldom reflect all of the elements of a representative transaction as defined by the term "fair market value."

SEC. 3. APPROACH TO VALUATION.

.01 A determination of fair market value, being a question of fact, will depend upon the circumstances in each case. No formula can be devised that will be generally applicable to the multitude of different valuation issues arising in estate and gift tax cases. Often, an appraiser will find wide differences of opinion as to the fair market value of a particular stock. In resolving such differences, he should maintain a reasonable attitude in recognition of the fact that valuation is not an exact science. A sound valuation will be based upon all the relevant facts, but the elements of common sense, informed judgment and reasonableness must enter into the process of weighing those facts and determining their aggregate significance.

.02 The fair market value of specific shares of stock will vary as general economic conditions change from "normal" to "boom" or "depression," that is, according to the degree of optimism or pessimism with which the investing public regards the future at the required date of appraisal. Uncertainty as to the stability or continuity of the future income from a property decreases its value by increasing the risk of loss of earnings and value in the future. The value of shares of stock of a company with very uncertain future prospects is highly speculative. The appraiser must exercise his judgment as to the degree of risk attaching to the business of the corporation which issued the stock, but that judgment must be related to all of the other factors affecting value.

.03 Valuation of securities is, in essence, a prophesy as to the future and must be based on facts available at the required date of appraisal. As a generalization, the prices of stocks which are traded in volume in a free and active market by informed persons best reflect the consensus of the investing public as to what the future holds for the corporations and industries represented. When a stock is closely held, is traded infrequently, or is traded in an erratic market, some other measure of value must be used. In many instances, the next best measure may be found in the prices at which the stocks of companies engaged in the same or a similar line of business are selling in a free and open market.

SEC. 4. FACTORS TO CONSIDER.

.01 It is advisable to emphasize that in the valuation of the stock of closely held corporations or the stock of corporations where market quotations are either lacking or too scarce to be recognized, all available financial data, as well as all relevant factors affecting the fair market value, should be considered. The following factors, although not all-inclusive are fundamental and require careful analysis in each case:

(a) The nature of the business and the history of the enterprise from its inception.

(b) The economic outlook in general and the condition and outlook of the specific industry in particular.

(c) The book value of the stock and the financial condition of the business.
(d) The earning capacity of the company.
(e) The dividend-paying capacity.
(f) Whether or not the enterprise has goodwill or other intangible value.

(g) Sales of the stock and the size of the block of stock to be valued.
(h) The market price of stocks of corporations engaged in the same or a similar line of business having their stocks actively traded in a free and open market, either on an exchange or over-the-counter.

.02 The following is a brief discussion of each of the foregoing factors:

(a) The history of a corporate enterprise will show its past stability or instability, its growth or lack of growth, the diversity or lack of diversity of its operations, and other facts needed to form an opinion of the degree of risk involved in the business. For an enterprise which changed its form of organization but carried on the same or closely similar operations of its predecessor, the history of the former enterprise should be considered. The detail to be considered should increase with approach to the required date of appraisal, since recent events are of greatest help in predicting the future; but a study of gross and net income, and of dividends covering a long prior period, is highly desirable. The history to be studied should include, but need not be limited to, the nature of the business, its products or services, its operating and investment assets, capital structure, plant facilities, sales records and management, all of which should be considered as of the date of the appraisal, with due regard for recent significant changes. Events of the past that are unlikely to recur in the future should be discounted, since value has a close relation to future expectancy.

(b) A sound appraisal of a closely held stock must consider current and prospective economic conditions as of the date of appraisal, both in the national economy and in the industry or industries with which the corporation is allied. It is important to know that the company is more or less successful than its competitors in the same industry, or that it is maintaining a stable position with respect to competitors. Equal or even greater significance may attach to the ability of the industry with which the company is allied to compete with other industries. Prospective competition which has not been a factor in prior years should be given careful attention. For example, high profits due to the novelty of its product and the lack of competition often lead to increasing competition. The public's appraisal of the future prospects of competitive industries or of competitors within an industry may be indicated by price trends in the markets for commodities and for securities. The loss of the manager of a so-called "one-man" business may have a depressing effect upon the value of the stock of such business, particularly if there is a lack of trained personnel capable of succeeding to the management of the enterprise. In valuing the stock of this type of business, therefore, the effect of the loss of the manager on the future expectancy of the business, and the absence of management-succession potentialities are pertinent factors to be taken into consideration. On the other hand, there may be factors which offset, in whole or in part, the loss of the manager's services. For instance, the nature of the business and of its assets may be such that they will not be impaired by the loss of the manager. Furthermore, the loss may be adequately covered by life insurance, or competent management might be employed on the basis of the consideration paid for the former manager's services. These, or other offsetting factors, if found to exist, should be carefully weighed against the loss of the manager's services in valuing the stock of the enterprise.

(c) Balance sheets should be obtained, preferably in the form of comparative annual statements for two or more years immediately preceding the date of appraisal, together with a balance sheet at the end of the month preceding that date, if corporate accounting will permit. Any balance sheet descriptions that are not self-explanatory, and balance sheet items comprehending diverse assets or liabilities, should be clarified in essential detail by supporting supplemental schedules. These statements usually will disclose to the appraiser (1) liquid position (ratio of current assets to current liabilities); (2) gross and net book value of principal classes of fixed assets; (3) working capital; (4) long-term indebtedness; (5) capital structure; and (6) net worth. Consideration also should be given to any assets not essential to the operation of the business, such as investments in securities, real estate, etc. In general, such nonoperating assets will command a lower rate of return than do the operating assets, although in exceptional cases the reverse may be true. In computing the book value per share of stock, assets of the investment type should be revalued on the basis of their market price and the book value adjusted accordingly. Comparison of the company's balance sheets over several years may reveal, among other facts, such developments as the acquisition of additional production facilities or subsidiary companies, improvement in financial position, and details as to recapitalizations and other changes in the capital structure of the corporation. If the corporation has more than one class of stock outstanding, the charter or certificate of incorporation should be examined to ascertain the explicit rights and privileges of the various stock issues including: (1) voting powers, (2) preference as to dividends, and (3) preference as to assets in the event of liquidation.

(d) Detailed profit-and-loss statements should be obtained and considered for a representative period immediately prior to the required date of appraisal, preferably five or more years. Such statements should show (1) gross income by principal items; (2) principal deductions from gross income including major prior items of operating expenses, interest and other expense on each item of long-term debt, depreciation and depletion if such deductions are made, officers' salaries, in total if they appear to be reasonable or in detail if they seem to be excessive, contributions (whether or not deductible for tax purposes) that the nature of its business and its community position require the corporation to make, and taxes by principal items, including income and excess profits taxes; (3) net income available for dividends; (4) rates and amounts of dividends paid on each class of stock; (5) remaining amount carried to surplus; and (6) adjustments to, and reconciliation with, surplus as stated on the balance sheet. With profit and loss statements of this character available, the appraiser should be able to separate recurrent from nonrecurrent items of income and expense, to distinguish between operating income and investment income, and to ascertain whether or not any line of business in which the company is engaged is operated consistently at a loss and might be abandoned with benefit to the company. The percentage of earnings retained for business expansion should be noted when dividend-paying capacity is considered. Potential future income is a major factor in many valuations of closely-held stocks, and all information concerning past income which will be helpful in predicting the future should be secured. Prior earnings records usually are the most reliable guide as to the future expectancy, but resort to arbitrary five-or-ten-year averages without regard to current trends or future prospects will not produce a realistic valuation. If, for instance, a record of progressively increasing or decreasing net income is found, then greater weight may be accorded the most recent years' profits in estimating earning power. It will be helpful, in judging risk and the extent to which a business is a marginal operator, to consider deductions from income and net income in terms of percentage of sales. Major categories of cost and expense to be so analyzed include the consumption of raw materials and supplies in the case of manufacturers, processors and fabricators; the cost of purchased merchandise in the case of merchants; utility services; insurance; taxes; depletion or depreciation; and interest.

(e) Primary consideration should be given to the dividend-paying capacity of the company rather than to dividends actually paid in the past. Recognition must be given to the necessity of retaining a reasonable portion of profits in a company to meet competition. Dividend-paying capacity is a factor that must be considered in an appraisal, but dividends actually paid in the past may not have any relation to dividend-paying capacity. Specifically, the dividends paid by a closely held family company may be measured by the income needs of the stockholders or by their desire to avoid taxes on dividend receipts, instead of by the ability of the company to pay dividends. Where an actual or effective controlling interest in a corporation is to be valued, the dividend factor is not a material element, since the payment of such dividends is discretionary with the controlling stockholders. The individual or group in control can substitute salaries and bonuses for dividends, thus reducing net income and understating the dividend-paying capacity of the company. It follows, therefore, that dividends are less reliable criteria of fair market value than other applicable factors.

(f) In the final analysis, goodwill is based upon earning capacity. The presence of goodwill and its value, therefore, rests upon the excess of net earnings over and above a fair return on the net tangible assets. While the element of goodwill may be based primarily on earnings, such factors as the prestige and renown of the business, the ownership of a trade or brand name, and a record of successful operation over a prolonged period in a particular locality, also may furnish support for the inclusion of intangible value. In some instances it may not be possible to make a separate appraisal of the tangible and intangible assets of the business. The enterprise has a value as an entity. Whatever intangible value there is, which is supportable by the facts, may be measured by the amount by which the appraised value of the tangible assets exceeds the net book value of such assets.

(g) Sales of stock of a closely held corporation should be carefully investigated to determine whether they represent transactions at arm's length. Forced or distress sales do not ordinarily reflect fair market value nor do isolated sales in small amounts necessarily control as the measure of value. This is especially true in the valuation of a controlling interest in a corporation. Since, in the case of closely held stocks, no prevailing market prices are available, there is no basis for making an adjustment for blockage. It follows, therefore, that such stocks should be valued upon a consideration of all the evidence affecting the fair market value. The size of the block of stock itself is a relevant factor to be considered. Although it is true that a minority interest in an unlisted corporation's stock is more difficult to sell than a similar block of listed stock, it is equally true that control of a corporation, either actual or in effect, representing as it does an added element of value, may justify a higher value for a specific block of stock.

(h) Section 2031(b) of the Code states, in effect, that in valuing unlisted securities the value of stock or securities of corporations engaged in the same or a similar line of business which are listed on an exchange should be taken into consideration along with all other factors. An important consideration is that the corporations to be used for comparisons have capital stocks which are actively traded by the public. In accordance with section 2031(b) of the Code, stocks listed on an exchange are to be considered first. However, if sufficient comparable companies whose stocks are listed on an exchange cannot be found, other comparable companies which have stocks actively traded in on the over-the-counter market also may be used. The essential factor is that whether the stocks are sold on an exchange or over-the-counter there is evidence of an active, free public market for the stock as of the valuation date. In selecting corporations for comparative purposes, care should be taken to use only comparable companies. Although the only restrictive requirement as to comparable corporations specified in the statute is that their lines of business be the same or similar, yet it is obvious that consideration must be given to other relevant factors in order that the most valid comparison possible will be obtained. For illustration, a corporation having one or more issues of preferred stock, bonds or debentures in addition to its common stock should not be considered to be directly comparable to one having only common stock outstanding. In like manner, a company with a declining business and decreasing markets is not comparable to one with a record of current progress and market expansion.

SEC. 5. WEIGHT TO BE ACCORDED VARIOUS FACTORS.

The valuation of closely held corporate stock entails the consideration of all relevant factors as stated in section 4. Depending upon the circumstances in each case, certain factors may carry more weight than others because of the nature of the company's business. To illustrate:

(a) Earnings may be the most important criterion of value in some cases whereas asset value will receive primary consideration in others. In general, the appraiser will accord primary consideration to earnings when valuing stocks of companies which sell products or services to the public; conversely, in the investment or holding type of company, the appraiser may accord the greatest weight to the assets underlying the security to be valued.

(b) The value of the stock of a closely held investment or real estate holding company, whether or not family owned, is closely related to the value of the assets underlying the stock. For companies of this type the appraiser should determine the fair market values of the assets of the company. Operating expenses of such a company and the cost of liquidating it, if any, merit consideration when appraising the relative values of the stock and the underlying assets. The market values of the underlying assets give due weight to potential earnings and dividends of the particular items of property underlying the stock, capitalized at rates deemed proper by the investing public at the date of appraisal. A current appraisal by the investing public should be superior to the retrospective opinion of an individual. For these reasons, adjusted net worth should be accorded greater weight in valuing the stock of a closely held investment or real estate holding company, whether or not family owned, than any of the other customary yardsticks of appraisal, such as earnings and dividend paying capacity.

SEC. 6. CAPITALIZATION RATES.

In the application of certain fundamental valuation factors, such as earnings and dividends, it is necessary to capitalize the average or current results at some appropriate rate. A determination of the proper capitalization rate presents one of the most difficult problems in valuation. That there is no ready or simple solution will become apparent by a cursory check of the rates of return and dividend yields in terms of the selling prices of corporate shares listed on the major exchanges of the country. Wide variations will be found even for companies in the same industry. Moreover, the ratio will fluctuate from year to year depending upon economic conditions. Thus, no standard tables of capitalization rates applicable to closely held corporations can be formulated. Among the more important factors to be taken into consideration in deciding upon a capitalization rate in a particular case are: (1) the nature of the business; (2) the risk involved; and (3) the stability or irregularity of earnings.

SEC. 7. AVERAGE OF FACTORS.

Because valuations cannot be made on the basis of a prescribed formula, there is no means whereby the various applicable factors in a particular case can be assigned mathematical weights in deriving the fair market value. For this reason, no useful purpose is served by taking an average of several factors (for example, book value, capitalized earnings and capitalized dividends) and basing the valuation on the result. Such a process excludes active consideration of other pertinent factors, and the end result cannot be supported by a realistic application of the significant facts in the case except by mere chance.

SEC. 8. RESTRICTIVE AGREEMENTS.

Frequently, in the valuation of closely held stock for estate and gift tax purposes, it will be found that the stock is subject to an agreement restricting its sale or transfer. Where shares of stock were acquired by a decedent subject to an option reserved by the issuing corporation to repurchase at a certain price, the option price is usually accepted as the fair market value for estate tax purposes. See Rev. Rul. 54–76, C.B. 1954–1, 194. However, in such case the option price is not determinative of fair market value for gift tax purposes. Where the option, or buy and sell agreement, is the result of voluntary action by the stockholders and is binding during the life as well as at the death of the stockholders, such agreement may or may not, depending upon the circumstances of each case, fix the value for estate tax purposes. However, such agreement is a factor to be considered, with other relevant factors, in determining fair market value. Where the stockholder is free to dispose of his shares during life and the option is to become effective only upon his death, the fair market value is not limited to the option price. It is always necessary to consider the relationship of the parties, the relative number of shares held by the decedent, and other material facts, to determine whether the agreement represents a bonafide business arrangement or is a device to pass the decedent's shares to the natural objects of his bounty for less than an adequate and full consideration in money or money's worth. In this connection see Rev. Rul. 157 C.B. 1953-2, 255, and Rev. Rul. 189, C.B. 1953-2, 294.

SEC. 9. EFFECT ON OTHER DOCUMENTS.

Revenue Ruling 54-77, C.B. 1954-1, 187, is hereby superseded.

(Also Part I, Section 170; 26 CFR 1.170-1.)   Rev. Proc. 66-49

A procedure to be used as a guideline by all persons making appraisals of donated property for Federal income tax purposes.

SECTION 1. PURPOSE.

The purpose of this procedure is to provide information and guidelines for taxpayers, individual appraisers, and valuation groups relative to appraisals of contributed property for Federal income tax purposes. The procedures outlined are applicable to all types of noncash property for which an appraisal is required such as real property, tangible or intangible personal property, and securities. These procedures are also appropriate for unique properties such as art objects, literary manuscripts, antiques, etc., with respect to which the determination of value often is more difficult.

SEC. 2. LAW AND REGULATIONS.

.01 Numerous sections of the Internal Revenue Code of 1954, as amended, give rise to a determination of value for Federal tax purposes; however, the significant section for purposes of this Revenue Procedure is section 170, Charitable, Etc., Contributions and Gifts.

.02 Value is defined in section 1.170-1(c) of the Income Tax Regulations as follows:

* * *. The fair market value is the price at which the property would change hands between a willing buyer and a willing seller, neither being under any compulsion to buy or sell and both having reasonable knowledge of relevant facts. * * *

.03 This section further provides that:

* * *. If the contribution is made in property of a type which the taxpayer sells in the course of his business, the fair market value is the price which the taxpayer would have received if he had sold the contributed property in the lowest usual market in which he customarily sells, at the time and place of contribution (and in the case of a contribution of goods in quantity, in the quantity contributed). * * *

.04 As to the measure of proof in determining the fair market value, all factors bearing on value are relevant including, where pertinent, the cost, or selling price of the item, sales of comparable properties, cost of reproduction, opinion evidence and appraisals. Fair market value depends upon value in the market and not on intrinsic worth.

.05 The cost or actual selling price of an item within a reasonable time before or after the valuation date may be the best evidence of its fair market value. Before such information is taken into account, it must be ascertained that the transaction was at arm's length and that the parties were fully informed as to all relevant facts. Absent such evidence, even the sales price of the item in question will not be persuasive.

.06 Sales of similar properties are often given probative weight by the courts in establishing fair market value. The weight to be given such evidence will be affected by the degree of similarity to the property under appraisal and the proximity of the date of sale to the valuation date.

.07 With respect to reproductive cost as a measure of fair market value, it must be shown that there is a probative correlation between the cost of reproduction and fair market value. Frequently, reproductive cost will be in excess of the fair market value.

.08 Generally, the weight to be given to opinion evidence depends on its origin and the thoroughness with which it is supported by experience and facts. It is only where expert opinion is supported by facts having strong probative value, that the opinion testimony will in itself be given appropriate weight. The underlying facts must corroborate the opinion; otherwise such opinion will be discounted or disregarded.

.09 The weight to be accorded any appraisal made either at or after the valuation date will depend largely upon the competence and knowledge of the appraiser with respect to the property and the market for such property.

SEC. 3. APPRAISAL FORMAT.

.01 When it becomes necessary to secure an appraisal in order to determine the values of items for Federal income tax purposes, such appraisals should be obtained from qualified and reputable sources, and the appraisal report should accompany the return when it is filed. The more complete the information filed with a tax return the more unlikely it will be that the Internal Revenue Service will find it necessary to question items on it. Thus, when reporting a deduction for charitable contributions on an income tax return, it will facilitate the review and the acceptance of the returned values if any appraisals which have been secured are furnished. The above-mentioned regulations prescribe that support of values claimed should be submitted and a properly prepared appraisal by a person qualified to make such an appraisal may well constitute the necessary substantiation. In this respect, it is not intended that all value determinations be supported by formal written appraisals as outlined in detail below. This is particularly applicable to minor items of property or where the value of the property is easily ascertainable by methods other than appraisal.

.02 In general, an appraisal report should contain at least the following:

(1) A summary of the appraiser's qualifications.

(2) A statement of the value and the appraiser's definition of the value he has obtained.

(3) The bases upon which the appraisal was made, including any restrictions, understandings, or covenants limiting the use or disposition of the property.

(4) The date as of which the property was valued.

(5) The signature of the appraiser and the date the appraisal was made.

.03 An example of the kind of data which should be contained in a typical appraisal is included below. This relates to the valuation of art objects, but a similar detailed breakdown can be outlined for any type of property. Appraisals of art objects, paintings in particular, should include:

(1) A complete description of the object, indicating the size, the subject matter, the medium, the name of the artist, approximate date created, the interest transferred, etc.

(2) The cost, date, and manner of acquisition.

(3) A history of the item including proof of authenticity such as a certificate of authentication if such exists.

(4) A photograph of a size and quality fully identifying the subject matter, preferably a 10″ x 12″ or larger print.

(5) A statement of the factors upon which the appraisal was based, such as:

(a) Sales of other works by the same artist particularly on or around the valuation date.

(b) Quoted prices in dealers' catalogs of the artist's works or of other artists of comparable stature.

(c) The economic state of the art market at or around the time of valuation, particularly with respect to the specific property.

(d) A record of any exhibitions at which the particular art object had been displayed.

(e) A statement as to the standing of the artist in his profession and in the particular school or time period.

.04 Although an appraisal report meets these requirements, the Internal Revenue Service is not relieved of the responsibility of reviewing appraisals to the extent deemed necessary.

SEC. 4. REVIEW OF VALUATION APPRAISALS.

.01 While the Service is responsible for reviewing appraisals, it is not responsible for making appraisals; the burden of supporting the fair market value listed on a return is the taxpayer's. The Internal Revenue Service cannot accord recognition to any appraiser or group of appraisers from the standpoint of unquestioned acceptance of their appraisals. Furthermore, the Service cannot approve valuations or appraisals prior to the actual filing of the tax return to which the appraisal pertains and cannot issue advance rulings approving or disapproving such appraisals.

.02 In determining the acceptability of the claimed value of the donated property, the Service may either accept the value claimed based on information or appraisals submitted with the return or make its own determination as to the fair market value. In either instance, the Service may find it necessary to:

(1) contact the taxpayer and ask for additional information,

(2) refer the valuation problem to a Service appraiser or valuation specialist,

(3) recommend that an independent appraiser be employed by the Service to appraise the asset in question. (This latter course is frequently used by the Service when objects requiring appraisers of highly specialized experience and knowledge are involved.)

The "formula" approach may be used in determining the fair market value of intangible assets of a business only if there is no better basis available for making the determination; A.R.M. 34, A.R.M. 68, O.D. 937, and Revenue Ruling 65-192 superseded.

SECTION 1001.—DETERMINATION OF AMOUNT OF AND RECOGNITION OF GAIN OR LOSS

26 CFR 1.1001-1: Computation of gain or loss. Rev. Rul. 68-609 [1]
(Also Section 167; 1.167(a)-3.)

The purpose of this Revenue Ruling is to update and restate, under the current statute and regulations, the currently outstanding portions of A.R.M. 34, C.B. 2, 31 (1920), A.R.M. 68, C.B. 3, 43 (1920), and O.D. 937, C.B. 4, 43 (1921).

The question presented is whether the "formula" approach, the capitalization of earnings in excess of a fair rate of return on net tangible assets, may be used to determine the fair market value of the intangible assets of a business

The "formula" approach may be stated as follows:

A percentage return on the average annual value of the tangible assets used in a business is determined, using a period of years (preferably not less than five) immediately prior to the valuation date. The amount of the percentage return on tangible assets, thus determined, is deducted from the average earnings of the business for such period and the remainder, if any, is considered to be the amount of the average annual earnings from the intangible assets of the business for the period. This amount (considered as the average annual earnings from intangibles), capitalized at a percentage of, say, 15 to 20 percent, is the value of the intangible assets of the business determined under the "formula" approach.

[1] Prepared pursuant to Rev. Proc. 67-6, C.B. 1967-1, 576.

The percentage of return on the average annual value of the tangible assets used should be the percentage prevailing in the industry involved at the date of valuation, or (when the industry percentage is not available) a percentage of 8 to 10 percent may be used.

The 8 percent rate of return and the 15 percent rate of capitalization are applied to tangibles and intangibles, respectively, of businesses with a small risk factor and stable and regular earnings; the 10 percent rate of return and 20 percent rate of capitalization are applied to businesses in which the hazards of business are relatively high.

The above rates are used as examples and are not appropriate in all cases. In applying the "formula" approach, the average earnings period and the capitalization rates are dependent upon the facts pertinent thereto in each case.

The past earnings to which the formula is applied should fairly reflect the probable future earnings. Ordinarily, the period should not be less than five years, and abnormal years, whether above or below the average, should be eliminated. If the business is a sole proprietorship or partnership, there should be deducted from the earnings of the business a reasonable amount for services performed by the owner or partners engaged in the business. See *Lloyd B. Sanderson Estate* v. *Commissioner*, 42 F. 2d 160 (1930). Further, only the tangible assets entering into net worth, including accounts and bills receivable in excess of accounts and bills payable, are used for determining earnings on the tangible assets. Factors that influence the capitalization rate include (1) the nature of the business, (2) the risk involved, and (3) the stability or irregularity of earnings.

The "formula" approach should not be used if there is better evidence available from which the value of intangibles can be determined. If the assets of a going business are sold upon the basis of a rate of capitalization that can be substantiated as being realistic, though it is not within the range of figures indicated here as the ones ordinarily to be adopted, the same rate of capitalization should be used in determining the value of intangibles.

Accordingly, the "formula" approach may be used for determining the fair market value of intangible assets of a business only if there is no better basis therefor available.

See also Revenue Ruling 59–60, C.B. 1959–1, 237, as modified by Revenue Ruling 65–193, C.B. 1965–2, 370, which sets forth the proper approach to use in the valuation of closely-held corporate stocks for estate and gift tax purposes. The general approach, methods, and factors, outlined in Revenue Ruling 59–60, as modified, are equally applicable to valuations of corporate stocks for income and other tax purposes as well as for estate and gift tax purposes. They apply also to problems involving the determination of the fair market value of business interests of any type, including partnerships and proprietorships, and of intangible assets for all tax purposes.

A.R.M. 34, A.R.M. 68, and O.D. 937 are superseded, since the positions set forth therein are restated to the extent applicable under current law in this Revenue Ruling. Revenue Ruling 65–192, C.B. 1965–2, 259, which contained restatements of A.R.M. 34 and A.R.M. 68, is also superseded.

---

26 CFR 1.1001–1: Computation of gain or loss.

Loan charges incurred by a seller to assist the purchaser of his house in obtaining a mortgage loan. See Rev. Rul. 68–650, page 78.

Rev. Proc. 77-12

SECTION 1. PURPOSE.

The purpose of this Revenue Procedure is to set forth guidelines for use by taxpayers and Service personnel in making fair market value determinations in situations where a corporation purchases the assets of a business containing inventory items for a lump sum or where a corporation acquires assets including inventory items by the liquidation of a subsidiary pursuant to the provisions of section 332 of the Internal Revenue Code of 1954 and the basis of the inventory received in liquidation is determined under section 334(b)(2). These guidelines are designed to assist taxpayers and Service personnel in assigning a fair market value to such assets.

SEC. 2. BACKGROUND.

If the assets of a business are purchased for a lump sum, or if the stock of a corporation is purchased and that corporation is liquidated under section 332 of the Code and the basis is determined under section 334(b)(2), the purchase price must be allocated among the assets acquired to determine the basis of each of such assets. In making such determinations, it is necessary to determine the fair market value of any inventory items involved. This Revenue Procedure describes methods that may be used to determine the fair market value of inventory items.

In determining the fair market value of inventory under the situations set forth in this Revenue Procedure, the amount of inventory generally would be different from the amounts usually purchased. In addition, the goods in process and finished goods on hand must be considered in light of what a willing purchaser would pay and a willing seller would accept for the inventory at the various stages of completion, when the former is not under any compulsion to buy and the latter is not under any compulsion to sell, both parties having reasonable knowledge of relevant facts.

SEC. 3. PROCEDURES FOR DETERMINATION OF FAIR MARKET VALUE.

Three basic methods an appraiser may use to determine the fair market value of inventory are the cost of reproduction method, the comparative sales method, and the income method. All methods of valuation are based on one or a combination of these three methods.

.01 The cost of reproduction method generally provides a good indication of fair market value if inventory is readily replaceable in a wholesale or retail business, but generally should not be used in establishing the fair market value of the finished goods of a manufacturing concern. In valuing a particular inventory under this method, however, other factors may be relevant. For example, a well balanced inventory available to fill customers' orders in the ordinary course of business may have a fair market value in excess of its cost of reproduction because it provides a continuity of business, whereas an inventory containing obsolete merchandise unsuitable for customers might have a fair market value of less than the cost of reproduction.

.02 The comparative sales method utilizes the actual or expected selling prices of finished goods to customers as a basis of determining fair market values of those finished goods. When the expected selling price is used as a basis for valuing finished goods inventory, consideration should be given to the time that would be required to dispose of this inventory, the expenses that would be expected to be incurred in such disposition, for example, all costs of disposition, applicable discounts (including those for quantity), sales commissions, and freight and shipping charges, and a profit commensurate with the amount of investment and degree of risk. It should also be recognized that the inventory to be valued may represent a larger quantity than the normal trading volume and the expected selling price can be a valid starting point only if customers' orders are filled in the ordinary course of business.

.03 The income method, when applied to fair market value determinations for finished goods, recognizes that finished goods must generally be valued in a profit motivated business. Since the amount of inventory may be large in relation to normal trading volume the highest and best use of the inventory will be to provide for a continuity of the marketing operation of the going business. Additionally, the finished goods inventory will usually provide the only source of revenue of an acquired business during the period it is being used to fill customers' orders. The historical financial data of an acquired company can be used to determine the amount that could be attributed to finished goods in order to pay all costs of disposition and provide a return on the investment during the period of disposition.

.04 The fair market value of work in process should be based on the same factors used to determine the fair market value of finished goods reduced by the expected costs of completion, including a reasonable profit allowance for the completion and selling effort of the acquiring corporation. In determining the fair market value of raw materials, the current costs of replacing the inventory in the quantities to be valued generally provides the most reliable standard.

Sec. 4. Conclusion.

Because valuing inventory is an inherently factual determination, no rigid formulas can be applied. Consequently, the methods outlined above can only serve as guidelines for determining the fair market value of inventories.

CHAPTER 12

POPULAR METHODS YOU SHOULD AVOID

There are a few methods in common use which are not recommended for trying to value a closely-held* or privately-held* business:

1- Comparable Sales Method
2- Price/Earnings Ratio Method
3- Replacement Cost Method
4- Rule-of-Thumb Pricing Methods traditionally used for certain types of businesses.

If you are interested, the basic procedure for each method is outlined below. Also discussed are the reasons for why each one is felt to be inappropriate. If you have heard of these techniques and are tempted to try to use them, it may be worthwhile to read these sections. Otherwise the rest of this chapter can be skipped.

Comparable Sales Method

This method attempts to equate the value of your subject company with the purchase prices of similar companies which have recently been sold. It assumes that their average sales price indicates what your company should sell for. Usually the sales prices of these "comparable companies" are boiled down to a "multiple* of after tax earnings", which supposedly should then be applied to the after tax earnings of your company to show its value. This is an acceptable theory, but the technique proves unworkable in practice most of the time. Comparable sales data may be a feasible method for valuing real estate, but it is an extremely ponderous procedure for valuing a business. It usually gets short-cut, and the results become unreliable in the process.

First of all, there is considerable question as to whether one company, or sales transaction, can ever really be considered comparable to another company or transaction. Businesses which seem very similar are always different in complex ways. To make this method reliable, you would have to make individual adjustments to the purchase price of each business in the comparison for each and every way it differs from the subject business. You have to compare apples and apples, not apples and oranges.

Here are some of the more obvious and significant ways in which companies and transactions differ:
- Physical facilities
- Type, amount, and quality of assets
- Internal differences regarding type and quality of management, policies affecting earnings, existence and terms of labor contracts, and so forth.
- The form and terms of the transaction. (See Chapter 14 for more on how this can affect price.)
- Uncontrollable differences in expenses which affect profitability (differing local wage scales, state taxes, local utility rates, etc.)
- Differences in how the purchase price was

paid. (Cash, stock, notes, earn-outs, installment sale, etc.)
- If stock of the purchasing company was traded for stock of the selling company, you also have to go back and value the buying company in order to know what its stock was worth at that time.
- Variation in the prevailing interest rate at the time of sale, which directly affects the rates of return used in the valuation, as well as the amount the buyer could afford to finance and pay.

For each company in the comparison you would have to calculate and make adjustments to the purchase price for each of these things.

There is an obvious problem in getting access to enough detailed information to be able to know all the significant ways in which the company differed from the subject business. Information on the form and terms of the transactions is equally difficult to uncover. And how are you going to be able to reliably predict what shape the transaction for the subject company is going to take? Following all this is the problem of determining what those differences are worth in money, and making all of the necessary adjustments to the sales price of the sample company to show what its sales price would have been if it had been just like the subject company. Keep in mind that you would have to do this for a sufficiently large sampling of companies, so that you end up with an average of many transactions. This is to help smooth out the differences resulting from the factors which you can't adjust for.

These are obviously complex, difficult, and time consuming calculations to make. The great subjectivity of the process makes it inherently less reliable. And digging up the required information can be next to impossible.

This is all compounded by the fact that only data on publicly-held companies is generally available for the comparison. Information regarding privately-held companies is closely guarded and there are no public disclosure rules which require its release. So what? Well, the problem is that public companies (and the deals concerning them) are completely different from privately-held and closely-held companies, so the data is often impossible to equate to the latter.

For one thing, a control premium is generally paid over and above the value of the stock when a publicly-held company is acquired. This is in order to reflect the added value that a majority stock interest has over that of a smaller interest. Also, publicly-held firms use different accounting methods than privately-held firms. To use the comparable sales method, you have to somehow go back and conform all of the income statements to the same accounting treatment used by the privately-held subject company, and then translate their effect on sales price.

Despite all this, it is useful to check out these comparable transactions insofar as the information is easily obtainable. If you are a buyer, this will give you an idea of what the seller's expectations regarding price may be. Companies in that industry group may have been selling at certain multiples of net profits consistently. If the details on these transactions and companies are available, study them so that you can point out the differences between them and the case at hand, and perhaps thereby justify a lower price than the seller expects.

On the other hand, if you are a seller, you could take the position that a consistent pattern of sales at a certain multiple is indicative of true market value. However, if the multiples from comparable companies vary all over the place, and you are trying to assert the use of an average of them, then this argument is weakened. It is going to boil down to the individual circumstances of the subject company. (Which means: use the other methods.) Going through the process of picking apart these other companies and deals should only serve to reinforce this point with the seller.

If you want to get involved with all this, the most authoritative source of data on other transactions is probably W.T. Grimm Co. (135 South LaSalle St., Chicago IL 60603). Industry associations can also be helpful.

All-in-all, these comparative valuations are easy to shoot down. If one party raises the issue of comparative transaction prices during negotiation, it is rather easy to blunt the impact of it by pointing out that such comparables serve as value indicators only to the extent that the companies and the transactions are truly comparable.

"Offers" to purchase a company are never reliable value indicators because they have not yet been fully negotiated at arms length. "Offers" change dramatically after going through the entire process leading to an actual acquisition agreement. They also suffer adjustments prior to, at, and after settlement. No buyer or seller should rely on these, or accept them as valid negotiating ammo.

Price/Earnings Ration Method (or "Multiple" of Earnings Method)

This method is similar to the Comparable Sales Method, only instead of looking to the past acquisition prices of "comparable" companies to get an average P/E (price/earnings) multiple, it looks at the current market price of publicly traded stocks for comparable companies. The technique suffers from the same basic limitations as the Comparable Sales Method, plus a few more when applied to a non-public company.

In this method, you determine the average Price/Earnings Ratio of the stock of publicly-traded companies which are similar to the company which you are valuing. Then you assume that the same P/E Ratio is valid for your company, and you use it to calculate what the market selling price of your company should be.

So, if:

P/E ratio for the stock of a publicly traded company = $\dfrac{\text{the stock's current traded price}}{\text{that company's Net Income After-Tax per share}}$

Then:
>That same P/E ratio
>
>X Your company's net income after-tax
>----
>= the market value of your company

The stock of larger companies tends to trade at higher P/E's than that of smaller companies. This is because, generally speaking, larger companies have proven to be more stable and reliable in their earnings. So a large company with the same earnings per share as a smaller company will trade at a higher price. In addition, the shares of a larger company are traded at a premium due to their increased marketability. Accordingly, the P/E ratio of a larger publicly-held company must be discounted prior to its application to a closely-held or privately-held situation.

Unlike the stock of a privately or closely-held firm, a public company's stock price is affected by factors other than that company's financial performance. The behavior of investors and of the market as a whole has a very great impact on any listed stock's price. This is why a company's stock price (and, hence, the "value" of that company) can vary tremendously from day to day. Therefore, "market value" may often seem an unfair indicator of true value. This puts the valuator into the predicament of having to speculate about what might occur if the subject company's stock were publicly traded. Another problem is that public shares represent fractional minority interests, and are not comparable to a 100% interest in the company being valued. A majority interest will always carry a per share premium.

By using this method for a privately-held company you are basically saying that the stock of this business is worth the same as that of the typical large publicly-held business in the same industry, assuming it had the same earnings. This is a pretty rash assumption. However, some basic input on the P/E ratios of stocks of "similar" companies which are publicly traded might prove valuable in bolstering some other point during price negotiations. Therefore, a reasonably efficient investigation into this may prove worthwhile.

However, this method can really only be substantiated as a valid valuation technique when the company being valued is a large publicly-held firm, with wide distribution of ownership and no major concentration of control of the outstanding stock in the hands of a small number of individuals or a particular group.

Note: There is one particular form of this method which should never be relied upon in any case (except perhaps as a general point of reference for comparing deals). This involves the use of a rule-of-thumb "multiple"*, which is multiplied times net after-tax earnings to give the value of the company.

This multiple (usually between 8 and 10) is supposed to correspond to the average return an investor would expect from an investment with similar risk. In most cases, users of this method pay no attention to the industry the company is in, or to the company's individual peculiarities, or to market conditions. They just apply a multiple of between 8 and 10, depending upon how successful the company seems to be. And they apply it directly to the net after tax earnings figure taken right off the income statement, without any adjustments whatsoever to the latter. This is probably the most unreliable, misleading way to value a company ever invented, yet somehow it still finds common use. It fails to consider any of the many, many individual factors which must have input into the valuation of any particular business.

The Replacement Cost Method

This method is really only used for insurance purposes, where the property is insured at "replacement value". Replacement cost of the entire company would reflect the value of recreating the entire business in terms of its tangible assets. It does not consider intangibles and it does not take into consideration the earning power of the business. Therefore, it overstates market value in some ways and understates value in other ways. The total end result is usually an overstatement. In most cases it would not be possible or economically realistic to try to duplicate a business in this manner anyway, except perhaps in the case of a brand-new "start up" concern which did not have any real business developed yet.

Rule-of-Thumb Methods Used For Particular Types of Businesses ("The Industry Method")

In many industries, particular little formulas have evolved to estimate the value of the businesses within them. They usually involve some form of "multiple", or gross revenue capitalization. In other words, average gross sales for a specific period (usually one month) are multiplied by a factor which has found acceptance in that particular industry. For example: 4 to 6 times gross monthly sales for a restaurant, or 10 to 12 times gross monthly sales for a retail clothing store, or 1.5 times annual commissions for an insurance agency. Generally, these formulas find their application in small retail or service businesses, and not in larger concerns or manufacturing companies.

For the types of companies which they are invented for, these rules-of-thumb might be useful starting places, but they are only general indicators for an "average" business in that field. They are an oversimplification and, therefore, should only be viewed as a very rough guide. They can provide a basic point of reference for comparing deals available within the same field. In that respect they have their place. For valuing something as important as a business, however, one of the more comprehensive methods should always be employed.

Contact the particular industry association for information on these methods. Also, the franchised or chain "business brokerage" firms usually supply their local offices with the formulas used for smaller retail and service businesses, since this is the bulk of their trade.

CHAPTER 13

SECURED LOAN VALUE

An Explanation of Secured Loan Value

Secured Loan Value tells you how much a lender will loan a buyer who uses the company's assets as collateral. The secured loan value of a company (its assets, that is) is a major factor in the determination of purchase price. If there aren't adequate assets present to borrow against in order to provide the bulk of the purchase price, the field of possible buyers is going to be slim. Therefore, the price often has to be tempered by the secured loan value present. Most buyers must qualify their deals based on whether sufficient assets are present to borrow against.

Of course, adequate collateral is not the only factor in the lending decision. Just as important, and sometimes more important, is the company's apparent ability to generate the cash necessary to "service" the loan (make the payments). The business has to be financially viable in its recapitalized form after the sale. No lender is interested in financing a bankruptcy or liquidation.

However, it is much harder to borrow solely against cash flow*, no matter how healthy the company is. A lender will usually make a loan in excess of the amount covered by the physical collateral only where there have been exceptional past earnings performance, an upward trend in sales, and very promising future prospects. For example, if the adjusted cash flow has been adequate in each of the past five year to <u>safely</u> make the loan payments which <u>would</u> have been necessary if the company had then been carrying the anticipated amount of debt, then a lender might consider making the loan in the absence of adequate collateral. But in other cases, the lender is necessarily limited by the nature, value, condition, and quality of the collateral assets, and these impose a definite limit on the size of the loan.

The lender's concern is with how much money it can get for the assets if the business fails and has to be liquidated. Secured loan value is generally somewhat less than liquidation value. This is due to the lender's traditional conservatism, the uncertainty regarding the actual amount of sales proceeds that will be received, and the expenses of conducting the sale. In fact, secured loan values are usually defined as a percentage of "orderly liquidation value" or "forced liquidation value". The former generally refers to an orderly sale of the assets within a six-month period, and for that reason it is closer to "market value". The latter refers to the amount which is likely to be received if the assets are disposed of at an auction sale held within a 60 day period. Since lenders do not want to be saddled with the burden of having to locate the best buyer, or with caring for and insuring the assets for any longer than they have to after they inherit them, an auction is the route that is usually taken. Forced liquidation value is therefore the preferred measure. In order to estimate secured loan value before an outside appraisal of the liquidation value of the assets is actually done, "book value" is of the assets is often used as a substitute. It is usually a bit lower than liquidation, and thus even more conservative.

The percentage which is applied to the value of the assets is called the "advance rate". To the extent that it is less than 100%, it reflects the lender's degree of confidence in the company's future success, the expected costs of conducting the liquidation, the relative liquidity* of the particular assets, and possible changes in the value of those assets.

Once the loan is made, the lender will require regular reports from the company, by which it monitors the continued presence and condition of the collateral. For instance, if the company has a revolving working capital loan secured by inventory, when those inventory levels drop, the lender must know this so that it can demand repayment of the principal to the extent that the agreed-upon security for it is no longer present.

<u>How to Determine Secured Loan Value</u>

Different types of assets have different advance rates. The actual rate used by the lender will depend upon the value, condition, desirability, and quality of the particular assets offered as security. Different types of lenders may use different rates as well. The only way to find out is to ask. As a general rule, however, the following advance rates can be expected:

<u>Type of Asset</u>	<u>Advance Rate</u>	X	<u>Measure of Value</u>
Accnts Receivable (minus doubtful accounts)	80%-90%		Book Value
Raw Materials Inventory	50%		Book Value
Finished Goods Inventory	25%-30%		Book Value
Work-In-Progress Inventory	0%-25%		Book Value
Machinery and Equipment	60%-80%		Liquidation Value
Real Estate	80%		Appraised Market Value

These assets are listed in their general order of desirability as security. There may be restrictions imposed by the lender regarding each class. For instance, obsolete equipment, or equipment designed to perform a specialized process, is often excluded from eligible collateral. Computers and other forms of electronic or high-tech equipment become obsolete so quickly that they are rarely accepted as collateral at the same advance rate as other equipment. Intangible assets are generally excluded altogether: (1) they are rarely worth anything once separated from the business, (2) there is usually no secondary market for their resale, (3) their value is difficult to estimate, and (4) even when it is pinned down, the value is often too nominal to have been worth the effort of estimating.

Using Accounts Receivable* As Loan Security

Any receivables older than 90 days are generally disqualified (unless 90 day terms are offered to customers as a standard practice in that particular industry). In addition, any "past due" receivables from an individual customer can disqualify all receivables from that customer. This is potentially disastrous for some companies.

Ineligible accounts receivable can sometimes be reincluded in the advance if sellers personally guarantee their collection, which they are often willing to do because it can result in a higher price for the company to that extent. Of course, the seller must have a high degree of confidence in the customer and its ability to pay. Receivables are typically used as security for revolving loans, such as those used to finance working capital.

Using Inventory As Loan Security

There is a great deal of variation in what can be advanced for inventory. The liquidation value of inventory can be close to zero in many industries, because the goods may have no real value to anyone else, and therefore only be worth their value as scrap. It all depends on the particular type of product being made. Raw material is more valuable if it is something that is widely used, such as sheet metal in standard sizes and gauges. Work-in-process is of little value to anyone except as scrap. Lenders will not generally take into consideration the fact the "WIP" might be pushed through to finished goods rather quickly. They make their loans based on the inventory as it stands at a normal point in time. They do not want to get involved in the complication of seeing that the stuff is converted to finished goods before they can get their money back.

The advance on finished goods depends upon the market for the product. It also depends on how much of the finished goods there are normally outstanding orders for. Some companies just pile up finished goods in quantities which are far out of proportion to the orders which they can anticipate within a reasonable length of time. Sellers who want a higher price will sometimes help a buyer obtain a larger loan advance by agreeing to buy back any unsold inventory.

Note that if the company uses the LIFO* (last in, first out) method of inventory accounting, there is likely to be a large amount of old inventory on the balance sheet at prices which are far below what it would be worth now. This hidden value can result in a higher advance rate.

Inventory is usually used as security for "revolving" type loans, such as those used to provide working capital. These are loans where the principal does not have to usually be paid back unless the security diminishes. Only the interest is paid. Accounts receivable are also used as security in combination with inventory for these loans. But since inventory is not as desireable as accounts receivable as security, the loan amount which is advanced against inventory is sometimes required to be paid back over time to some extent (amortized*). It depends on how confident the lender is about the quality of the security and about the company's future.

Using Machinery and Equipment As Loan Security

The value of machinery and equipment is generally based on forced liquidation value because of its relative lack of liquidity. It is almost always sold at auction. Anyone who has purchased equipment through a used equipment dealer is familiar with the kind of savings which can be had. Most of what they stock is purchased at auction and marked up accordingly, so the extreme discount from original cost to secured loan value is understandable.

Several factors go into the determination of the advance rate and whether a certain piece of equipment of eligible as security. Equipment which is obsolete or subject to rapid technological change is likely to be excluded. Equipment will be less valuable as security if it is designed to perform a specialized function or process. This is because there will be fewer potential buyers for the item, and perhaps none at all. The number of prospective buyers also slims quite a bit when the particular piece is relatively expensive. Also of concern is whether the item can be easily detached and moved from the premises. If this process is costly or complicated, it will detract significantly from value. Lenders will also consider the overall vitality of the specific industry to which the equipment pertains. This bears on the resale demand for such equipment.

Remember that the lender will require a current appraisal of these assets by an independent, professional appraiser. Most are capable of giving an accurate appraisal if they are merely supplied with a complete description of all the assets: type, model, cost, depreciation taken, and condition. However, as a rule they will not do this. They insist upon a physical inspection in order to verify the existence and condition of the assets. Fortunately, appraisals will often show that equipment values are understated on the balance sheet, due to the effects of depreciation deductions and inflation. However, make sure that the appraisal is prepared specifically for market and liquidation values, and not replacement value. The latter is used for insurance purposes and it is not acceptable to lenders.

Equipment is generally used as security for term loans, and the term is usually rather short (around 5 years) unless the equipment is combined with real estate as security for a longer term loan.

Using Real Estate As Loan Security

Much to the surprise of many borrowers, real estate is perhaps the least attractive form of security for an acquisition loan, and this is due to its unpredictable marketability. Real estate demand fluctuates constantly. A real estate purchase is always a large one which requires financing, so the state of the economy and the current interest rates also end up having a significant and unpredictable impact on saleability at any given time. Furthermore, industrial buildings always have a limited market. There aren't that many industrial property buyers out there. If the building has been designed or altered to suit the particular processes used by that company, then it will be even harder to sell. If it is a commercial structure such as an office building, it may not be attractive as security either, because the lender has no desire to get involved with finding and maintaining tenants for the building, and then managing it during the period before it is sold. And buyers for a single-user commercial building are just as hard to find as industrial buyers. The lender also gets stuck with the inevitable expenses of maintaining the building physically.

For all of these reasons, lenders do not like to inherit real estate. Consequently, if the company's prospects for success after the acquisition are less than glowing, the lender may refuse to advance against real estate at all. More likely, however, is that the lender will combine the real estate with the other fixed assets as security for a single amount which is really only advanced against the value of those other assets. They frame the loan amount as one being advanced against the whole group of assets according to an undisclosed formula, but actually you may not be getting much of an advance at all for the real estate. It is just thrown in for added security.

Real estate, however, is appealing security for "seller financing". The seller generally has much more confidence in the desirability and value of the real estate than the typical asset based lender. The factors which bother the other lenders are not as much of a problem for a seller, who is better equipped and more willing to handle them. A seller will often become the real estate lender by taking back a note secured by a first mortgage on the property. Alternatively, a buyer can purchase all of the assets of the company except the real estate, whose title remains with the seller, and then lease the property from the seller, with or without an option to purchase at some future date. Private sellers tend to be more real estate oriented and more apt to be attracted to such an arrangement.

Often, for tax purposes, a buyer will purchase the property personally, and lease it to his newly acquired company. In this case, the personal credit of the individual becomes as important as the credit of the "tenant".

Real estate is generally appraised at market value by an "MAI" certified real estate appraiser. Some lenders will accept an average of a number of informal estimates of market value made by real estate agencies. A few telephone calls to these firms should result in the necessary feedback, but always ask for their replies on their letterhead. Be honest and tell them that you are not interested in listing the property, but that you need the figure for other reasons. They will often do this as a gesture of good will in the hope that you will remember them when later real estate needs arise. It is an expenditure of their time, however, and they should be given the facts so that they have the opportunity to decline if they see fit. Nonetheless, be careful about disclosing your precise plans, because rumors can run rampant on these things and your confidential plans may not be confidential for long.

Important Limit on Secured Loan Value

Once you have calculated what the total collateral value of the assets will be, you still must determine whether the business will generate the cash flow needed to make the anticipated loan payments. You can only borrow an amount which you can repay. See Chapter 15 (on Cash Flow Analysis) for instructions on this.

If necessary, see Step 4 of Chapter 6 for details on how to predict the types and amounts of loans which will possibly be used to finance the acquisition.

CHAPTER 14

SOME FINAL POINTS TO CONSIDER IN WRAPPING UP THE VALUATION

At this point you should have gone through and conducted your valuation according to several different methods. The results from each will probably be very different, indicating a range of possible values for the company. Your job now is to narrow that range down and refine your final estimate of value. This is a rather subjective process. Just have good reasons to justify what you conclude. Read through this chapter for input on your final decisions, and pay particular attention to the final two sections.

Try To Be Objective and Realistic

This is a sensitive topic and sellers should try hard not to be turned off by it. However, it is not uncommon for sellers to somehow develop the idea that there are a lot of rich corporate buyers out there who are just dying to pay too much for acquisitions. Sellers who do so are really doing themselves a dis-service. An unwillingness to face reality on the subject of value can be damaging for several reasons. First of all is the tremendous waste of a great deal of very precious time, not only by the seller, but by well intended buyers too. It's amazing how much time is consumed even in the preliminary stages of acquisition discussions, and it's all in vain if the price is too high, because the deal just won't go. At the same time, the seller often suffers a loss of credibility in the business community as his stance becomes commonly known.

The company can be damaged as well by being on the market for too long and thereby gaining a shopworn, undesirable appearance - warranted or not. Another effect may be that the sale is delayed to a time when the company is not performing as well as it was before, or to a time when the market for such an acquisition is not as attractive, both of which serve to lower the price that is eventually received for the business.

It is important for the seller to view the company as if he were acquiring it himself. If it was his competitor's company, would he pay that high a price? It's tough to be objective about something so close to you, but this is one time when it is important to do so. Contrary to a slogan of one of the business brokerage chains, a common problem for sellers isn't that they run a danger of giving their company away, it's just the opposite - they often damage themselves and their firm by insisting for too long on an unrealistically high price.

Negotiation Will Affect Final Price

Negotiation involves give and take. The buyer and seller's viewpoints on price will vary and some compromise will be necessary in order to bring them together on a deal. Since the objectives of each side are different, the company will have a different value to both of them. The possibility of resolving such differences depends upon the relative desire of each to sell and to buy.

Just remember that price is not the only important term in the agreement that needs to be negotiated. Each side has other things to trade off if price is that great a concern to them. Horse trading tactics don't seem to go far in acquisitions, so before negotiation really begins each side will be flushed out to a reasonable opening stance on price. This usually happens as soon as they are faced with having to actually justify their initial position.

Value the Company As It Stands Now

It is often said that valuation reflects the present worth of a future flow of earnings. While this is true, the future should be forecast only with reference to the present. In very few cases can it be said with certainty that the future will actually outperform the past, and it is therefore considered inappropriate to assume that sales will be any higher than they are right now, or that management is not currently operating at peak performance. In other words, don't base your valuation on a hypothetical pro forma* income statement. Base it only on current results. Use an adjusted statement which reflects only common-sense changes which can be quantified with certainty. Try to remember that if better results are obtained in the future, it will actually be the buyer's doing, and the seller can only really expect to be paid for what he has actually done to date himself. If the seller sees a good trend ahead, and wants it reflected in the price he gets for his company, then perhaps he should retain ownership a bit longer to take advantage of it.

Those who do prepare pro formas or forecasts for use by others should be very careful, for they can be viewed as vouching for their achievability. Many bad deals have been motivated solely by overly optimistic sales forecasts. Even if everything else goes right, forecasts can always get thrown off by uncontrollable costs, employee relations, government controls, tax law changes, and the general condition of the economy. Remember also that, in valuation, future profits usually must be discounted to present value.

There are rare situations in which higher future earnings might be taken into consideration in setting the purchase price. But since they are still always speculative, any amount of additional payment (over what the company's present earnings say it is worth) should be paid only on a contingent basis. That is, <u>if</u> the increased earnings actually appear, then the seller is paid more. This is known as an "earn out". An example might be in the case where the company has just discovered a new patented process which it feels will raise sales and earnings, but it has not had time to experience these benefits yet.

<u>Divorce Situations</u>

The value of a business must often be adjusted downward where it is being sold pursuant to a divorce settlement. One common reason is because an exiting spouse takes indispensible knowledge or abilities with them. They may have been a vital factor in the company's success. In fact, sometimes the business actually has to be dismantled because it can't run without that person.

The business may also have to be broken up to some extent in order to provide for a property settlement. Try to get a idea for what assets may have to be sold in order to make the settlement, or whether it can be sold as a whole and the proceeds split.

<u>Where The Bulk of the Company's Assets Is Inventory</u>

In this case there is a danger for the buyer that inventory will be allowed to shrink below normal levels after the agreement is signed, but prior to settlement. If the agreement is well drafted, it will provide for an adjustment of the purchase price in this case, pursuant to an audit of inventory on the day prior to closing.

Intermediaries involved in the transaction can also be unfairly hurt in such a case, because their compensation is based on actual purchase price, which may shrink dramatically. They should anticipate this possibility and take some steps to preserve the integrity of their fee.

Sellers should always take a close look at inventory, and adjust for obsolete or unusable stock.

Get An Accountant to Check Over Your Work Before You Rely Upon It

Before you make any actual decisions in reliance upon your valuation work, have your accountant review it. Since you have already pulled it all together and done the calculations, it should not take much for the accountant to go over it. But there are a lot of little things which can be misunderstood or overlooked. Make sure you have recorded all of your assumptions along the way. This manual can not take the place of an accountant in that regard, and does not purport to.

Even if you are a professional who is preparing the valuation for someone else, get the client's CPA into the act in order to verify your raw data, assumptions, and calculations. Defer to the accountant in your disclaimer, and state that you have depended solely upon the company or client for the necessary input. Always advise the client to consult a tax specialist. Taxes are a volatile area in which the client must have reliable, up to date advice.

Deduct Any Liabilities Which A Buyer Would Assume

Have all of the liabilities (and potential liabilities) being assumed by the buyer been recognized, and the purchase price adjusted accordingly? The buyer should always have a legal review done to check out things like tax obligations, contractual obligations, labor union contracts, potential litigation, and employee bonus, profit sharing or pension plans. The latter must usually be maintained after the acquisition in order to preserve employee relations, yet they may carry huge potential liabilities with them since they may be significantly underfunded by the former employer. Defined benefit pension plans, particularly the multi-employer variety which many parent companies maintain, are something buyers <u>and sellers</u> should always be wary of.

Sellers should think ahead before ever getting involved with such benefit plans, because they can end up developing a huge liability without even being aware of it. This is an area in which they can really get hammered. When the assets or stock of a company is sold, the pension plan can be deemed to have been terminated. The plan is then frozen and the seller can be liable for all of the unfunded liabilities of the plan. This amount can exceed the proceeds of sale. Instead of retiring to Florida to go fishing, he ends up in the poor house. The government commissions which assess these liabilties tend to be very unsympathetic to your pleas that you didn't know what you were getting into. Always consult an attorney specializing in pension plans.

Can The Business Pay For Itself At The Assumed Price?

If you are a buyer, remember that the business generally must be able to pay for itself out of its own cash flow over a reasonable length of time, with a reasonable safety cushion present. Unless the company has some other special value which justifies otherwise, this is the bottom line for a buyer who finances the purchase price, as most do. See Chapter 15 for more on this.

Where the Buyer Pays With Its Own Stock

If the buyer trades its own stock for the stock of the selling company, the seller has to determine what that stock is worth by valuing the buying company (unless it is publicly traded, so that the stock price can be easily found). Note that it should be based upon what the buyer's business will be worth <u>after</u> the acquisition. Often investment banking firms will conduct valuations specifically for this purpose. When these are used to determine the fairness of the price offered for the stock of minority shareholders by way of a tender offer, they are known as "fairness opinions". They are usually only undertaken when there is a dispute or if a very large amount is at issue.

<u>Squaring the Results From the Different Methods (Correlation of Results)</u>

By this point you should have determined the value of the company using as many of the different methods as possible. All of the results will be different, and the difference between them may be quite substantial. Some methods will apply better to your company than others, and those should be accorded more weight. What you should really have, however, is a <u>range</u> of possible values. No single number is absolutely correct, but you should be able to narrow it down quite a bit just by using common sense. If a method which did not really apply that well to your situation produced a very high or very low number, it is probably best to discard it from consideration.

So your first step is to refine the range, based upon how well certain methods fit your case from a theoretical standpoint, as opposed to others. After you have done that, there are further adjustments which you should make, based on the presence of certain other factors which typically influence what the final sale price of a company will be. Some of the more common ones are discussed in the following section. These further refine where within the range the price or value is likely to be. However, depending on which ones and how many of them come into play, they may even carry the ultimate price completely outside of the range. Therefore, don't necessarily think of that range as representing the absolute ceiling and bottom line figures.

Perhaps the best way to approach it is to try to zero in on the most likely value within your range, based solely on the relative applicability of the different methods. Then adjust it from there based upon the factors discussed below. Chances are, you will still end up within the range.

If you are not actually preparing for a sale of the company, then there is obviously a lot less to think about. But, even in that case, some of these factors still have to be dealt with, because the value you are aiming for is "market value", and market value always assumes the sale of the company.

On the other hand, it is really tough to predict what "dollar effect" a certain factor is actually going to have. You'll just have to use your judgment. Now you should be starting to understand that business valuation is a very imprecise thing. Oddly enough, this is one field in which even those with years of experience are not able to reliably predict what effect a given factor may have on price or value. That is why expensive valuations done by such firms still always have limited value.

All valuation can really do is give you an idea of "about" what the value of your company is. It can give you a "hoped for" value. It gives you an "argument" for what it may be worth under certain circumstances. It can let you know what the other possibilities might be, and what factors are going to affect where the price really ends up if it gets fully negotiated as part of a deal. It can give you a benchmark for comparing other companies valued by the same method. And valuing the same company periodically, according to the same method, can tell you how the company has grown or declined from a relative point of view. But it can't tell you exactly what it's worth, and don't believe anyone who tells you otherwise. It's so nebulous, so imprecise, so subjective. Where parties agree in advance that a certain <u>method</u> of determining value shall be adhered to for the purpose of their situation, then you can at least "assume" that you have ended up where you should have. But that's about as close as you get to certainty in valuation. Even then, the subjectivity within each method is still going to give you plenty to differ over.

Other Factors in a Transaction Which Will Affect the Purchase Price

Establishing a value for a business is not the same as setting a price for selling that business. The following is a list of factors which might enhance or diminish the final number as it is finally negotiated.

- <u>Will the transaction take the form of a purchase of assets or a purchase of stock?</u> - An asset deal is generally more favorable to the buyer, because he is able to avoid the prior liabilities of the company. It also enables him to start out with an entirely new depreciation schedule for tax purposes. (See Chapter 6, Step 3; and Chapter 5, Step 3b) (This can also be done where the company is acquired by purchasing the stock - using Section 338 of the Internal Revenue Code. But tax laws change frequently, so see your accountant.) The greater the depreciation a company can annually deduct, the greater its cash flow. And all buyers want to see good cash flow.

In stock deals not qualifiying under Section 338, the buyer inherits the old, more fully depreciated asset schedule (as well as the other tax attributes of the corporation). This is because that corporation remains intact after the deal, and it is that corporate entity which the buyer is buying. If an asset costing $50,000 has been completely written off except for $1000, then that's all the depreciation the new owner will ever be able to take on it too.

On the other hand, an asset buyer either forms a new corporation to acquire the assets, or acquires them through another previously existing corporation. And similar to when that corporation buys new property, it gets to start from scratch and depreciate it based on its full purchase cost.

In an asset deal, unless it qualifies as a parital or total liquidation under the Internal Revenue Code, the seller generally gives up more favorable capital gain treatment on the sale proceeds, and also may have to recapture some prior depreciation deductions as ordinary income. However, if most of the assets of the company are older and rather fully depreciated, the seller usually has no choice but to offer an asset sale, for no buyer would consider it under any other terms. With the large load of acquisition financing carried by the company after settlement, the buyer will need the additional cash flow which higher depreciation can provide in order for the corporation to be financially viable in its post-acquisition form. In that case, the seller is not in a position to ask for more purchase price from the buyer in exchange for giving up those tax advantages. But if the current depreciation schedule provides a healthy deduction and still has a long way to go before becoming exhausted, it becomes more of a negotiable point.

- <u>In a stock sale, the buyer acquires all of the seller's unknown and undisclosed liabilities.</u> What are the risks here? Just knowing that there will not be hidden liabilities cropping up is worth something to some buyers, so they will give in a little bit on price to get an asset deal. On the other hand, if the company has had a history of legal problems, or if products liability problems are common in that particular industry, the seller may have to offer an asset deal, or some type of legal indemnification, before any buyer will get involved.

- <u>In an asset sale, how will the purchase price be allocated*?</u> - Price allocations which benefit one party a great deal more than the other may justify an adjustment of the sales price. Both parties are committed to the same allocation. Usually, however, the allocation is a compromise and no adjustment is made to price.

For instance, if there is no goodwill value in the company, yet the parties agree to allocate part of the purchase price to goodwill, the seller will receive a tax benefit which he would otherwise not enjoy. This is because profits attributed to the sale of goodwill are treated as capital gain rather than ordinary income. However, by agreeing to this the buyer incurs a detriment because the "goodwill" he has acquired is not a depreciable asset under the tax laws. This would justify some price adjustment which favors the buyer.

- <u>If it is a stock sale, will a net operating loss carryover be inherited by the buyer?</u> This means the company has sustained losses to such an extent that it has not had sufficient income to even write them off against. Companies in this situation do not generally have high values to begin with. Often the assets of the firm are sold separately, with the proceeds distributed to the stockholders, and the empty corporate shell (still retaining the tax loss carryforward) is sold to a different party. The price is determined by the discounted value of the tax benefit available to the buyer. See your accountant on this because there are restrictions on the use of a tax loss carryforward by a different business.

- <u>Seller Financing</u> - Where the seller offers an installment sale at better terms than the buyer can get from conventional sources, the buyer has obtained a benefit which he ought to be willing to pay a bit more for. But it depends on the terms. The fact that the seller offers to finance the deal may not in itself warrant a higher price, because the seller also receives a great advantage in such an arrangement. The seller here receives a tax benefit, from having the profit from the sale spread out over a number of years rather than being received in one large lump sum. But, depending on the buyer, he may be assuming a very great risk by financing the deal himself.

So, depending on the credit-worthiness of the buyer, the buyer and the seller may be receiving offsetting benefits. If that is the case, to warrant something more from the buyer, the seller must provide much better terms than those offered by commercial lenders, or else finance the price on an unsecured basis. If the terms are only slightly better, both sides get an advantage and it's a wash. One side has not incurred a detriment for sake of the other party.

In many cases, the seller <u>must</u> offer financing in order to make up for other problems inherent in the company. Sometimes the seller has no choice, because the company's cash flow is not adequate to support the costs of conventional financing at a price acceptable to the seller.

There are additional adjustments which might be made due to seller financing. For instance, the smaller the down payment, the better the deal for the buyer, so the price agreed on up to that point might be adjusted upward a bit in order to compensate the seller. The normal downpayment is 10% to 20%. (In the past, there have been limits imposed by IRS on how large the amount paid in the first year can be, beyond which the special tax status of an installment sale is lost. Check the current tax code.) In addition, the more security the seller demands for the unpaid price, the lower the price he is going to command from the buyer.

- <u>Interest Rates and Available Loan Terms</u> - When the buyer's cost of financing is less, he can usually afford to pay more purchase price. Therefore, the potential price of a company can actually fluctuate along with market interest rates and the economy.

- <u>Are the assets so old that they are fully depreciated,</u> thus showing low depreciation charges against profits on the income statement, so that profits are overstated? The income statement really has to be adjusted to show the realistic post-acquisition depreciation charges. (See Chapter 5, Step 3; Chapter 6, Step 3; and Chapter 3)

- The size of the asset base. - Are there adequate assets available to provide collateral for secured financing of the entire purchase price? Or does the asset base fall short, thereby requiring the buyers to put their personal assets at stake as collateral? - or requiring too much unsecured financing or equity financing to make the deal attractive? The only way around this may be to adjust the purchase price downward.

- Is less than the majority of the stock being transferred? - A block of stock which conveys only a minority voting interest will command less per share. The purchase price calculated in valuation generally assumes that control of the company will be transferred.

- Stock as the buyer's method of payment - Buyers do not like to lay out cash for acquisitions, so they are often willing to offer a higher price if it can be paid for in stock. Sometimes the transaction can be arranged as a "tax-free exchange", so that the seller does not have to recognize any taxable gain immediately on the sale of the company. He only does so later, when he sells the stock he received. However, the stock can be difficult to sell, reducing the seller's financial liquidity*, and there is also a risk that it will decrease in value in the meantime. If there is a tax-free exchange of stock, there are also restrictions imposed by the Securities Exchange Commission on how soon the stock can be resold after the transaction. These must be adhered to, or the tax-free status of the deal will be lost and the seller will end up with a hefty tax bill. Therefore, the receipt of stock almost always justifies a higher price for the seller.

- Is a high priced stock being offered as the payment medium? - With many publicly-traded stocks, market enthusiasm drives the price of the stock well beyond its earnings value. Such stocks are referred to as "overpriced", and their market price usually drops (suffers a "market adjustment") not long thereafter.

If the seller is receiving such a stock as the payment medium, then perhaps the price demanded for the company should be as inflated as the market value of that stock is over its "earnings value".

- <u>Are there contingent price features in the deal</u>, so that some amount of the purchase price may be paid only if certain events occur? One common term is an "earn out", whereby post-acquisition profits exceeding a certain level result in additional payments to the seller. These occur when the seller wants a price that is based on higher future earnings which he feels are certain to occur, yet the buyer isn't as convinced. While these arrangements provide protection and additional compensation for the seller, they are a burden for the buyer and justify a lower price paid at settlement.

- <u>Can part of the purchase price be structured as an employment or consulting contract for the seller?</u> - This allows the buyer to treat part of the purchase price as a tax deductible salary expense, and also to defer part of its payment to the future. Often the seller is not really expected to do much at all to earn this compensation, other than helping with the normal post-acquisition transition over to new management. On the other hand, this arrangement bestows a benefit on the seller as well as the buyer, by allowing the receipt of the purchase price to be spread out more, thus lessening the overall tax bite. Whether or not it affects purchase price can be a toss up. Perhaps it could result in a price adjustment to the detriment of the party who requests the arrangement, if the other side plays its cards right.

- <u>Will present management remain after the sale?</u>
This is less often a benefit which the seller extends to the buyer than it is a condition of there being any deal at all. If the continued success of the business is dependent upon the special talents, contacts, or abilities of the individuals currently running the company, then the business is worth less if they plan to leave after the acquisition. In most cases they

have to stay for a certain period of time anyway in order to insure a smooth transition over to new management. On the other hand, if the buyer planned on assuming an active role in the management of the business which would displace the current management, or if it had other managers it wanted to bring in, then management's willingness to stay represents no advantage. But, in many cases, one of the first questions a prospective buyer asks, as a condition to having any interest in the deal at all, is whether management will stay. In that situation, it is tough for the seller to parlay staying into some price advantage. And if the management concerned includes persons other than the sellers, the seller may have no control over it at all.

Strategically, the best thing that can be done by a seller whose continued presence is in issue, is to say that it is a negotiable item, and hope to be able to continue to defer an answer on it until a basic price, not contingent upon the seller staying, has been agreed upon. The buyer, on the other hand, would be wise to resolve the issue first, and make it a condition of any offer made at a certain price.

For the buyer, if it is assumed that the present management will stay, what is the long-term assessment of the abilities of that group? Is it felt that they will have to be replaced? If so, this is a costly project that will detract from the present value of the company by the additional amount it would cost to put the preferred people in there. Does the company need more management than is currently in place? Increasingly, buyers want companies which can run themselves. Having to manage a subsidiary or investment acquisition is a negative factor for them. And, especially with larger buyers, it's not a lack of ability in the present managers, but having the same management philosophy, that leads to replacement of managers by others who have been previously indoctrinated with the buyer's way of thinking.

- <u>Is a "covenant not to compete" from the seller included in the deal?</u> This is a standard item. If a seller refuses to provide one, it will severely lessen the price he can get for his company. In fact, few buyers would consider the deal at all without one, faced with the prospect of the seller embarking on a competing business venture after the acquisition.

- <u>Is a union present?</u> - The presence of a union in inevitably interpreted as a disadvantage by the buyer. A seller whose employees are represented by a union can expect a lower price for that company than would be obtained for a similar company without one. Many buyers will not go near a company whose employees are represented by a union.

- <u>What are the prospects for the industry as a whole?</u> - No matter what the market position or profitability is of the company itself, its overall value will be affected by the future outlook for its industry as a whole. All else being equal, a business in a growing industry is worth more than one in a declining field.

Talk to competitors and trade associations. Consult Robert Morris Associates (Philadelphia), and publications such as Value Line, Standard & Poors, and Moody's for their evaluations of the particular industry. Assess the effect of anticipated technological change on the industry. Look at the trends.

- <u>What is the current state of the economy?</u> - Few industries or companies are immune from the influence of external economic factors. The fortunes of many companies rise and fall in direct relationship to the cycles of recession, inflation, and fluctuating interest rates. It doesn't seem fair, but the company could be worth less simply because of timing with the state of the economy. Pay attention to trends and forecasts regarding this factor.

- <u>Do conditions, expenses, or competition in the local market</u> make this company worth more or less than a similar one located somewhere else?

- <u>Do extraordinary capital expenditures or research & development expenditures need to be made in the future?</u> How much corrective action is needed by the buyer?

How about product development? This factor is best compensated for by adjusting the income statement on which the valuation is based so that it reflects the added costs. But if this item was missed before the calculations were done then the end result should be adjusted. Buyers should especially look for routine capital expenditures and maintenance which should have been performed but which have instead been deferred or skipped over in anticipation of the sale of the company, in order to reduce income statement expenses and thereby improve apparent financial performance.

- How do the company's financial ratios look?
It is important to assess the trends in these indicators over several years.

- Are all of the facts disclosed? - The buyer who commits himself in any way while the seller is holding back is asking for trouble. If for some reason an offer is made on the basis of incomplete data, it not only should contain contingencies, it should be at a lower number which reflects the added risk involved. The seller should expect that any intelligent buyer is going to do this, and that the offers received are going to reflect this wariness. The seller is going to do a lot better on price if he opens up.

- How much competition does the company face? - Profitability is generally held down in more competitive industries, since companies tend to be more cut-throat. Naturally, potential for profitability has a direct impact on value.

- Is there some special synergy or competitive advantage which will come to the buyer as a result of the acquisition? - This generally increases the value of the acquisition to that particular buyer. The buyer who will pay the highest price is the one who can gain some unusual enhancement of his existing business by integrating the acquired company's operations with it.

- <u>Does the company have a proprietary interest in its product or service?</u> - In other words, does it own the rights to some aspect of it, or does it have protective agreements, so that it is insulated from the effects of competition in some respects, and can control its prices better than others? This always adds value.

- <u>A buyer which is a publicly listed corporation generally will not pay</u> a price which represents a multiple of earnings greater than its own stock's P/E multiple. This is because, unless the acquisition is relatively small, the deal dilutes the buyer's own reported earnings per share, thus affecting its performance negatively in the eyes of the investment community.

These are only some of the more obvious factors which can affect value or negotiated price. There are scores of other transaction terms, transfer techniques, tax treatments, and other conditions which determine the bottom-line benefits to the parties in a deal. A full treatment of every conceivable factor is beyond the scope of this book, but make sure you consult an attorney and an accountant early in the course of any deal you become involved with so that you are properly advised of such concerns when and if they become potentially applicable to your deal.

<u>Finally:</u> If you are a buyer valuing a company which you are interested in acquiring, remember to go to Chapter 15 in order to test whether the company will be able to pay for itself out of its own cash flow if purchased at the assumed price.

CHAPTER 15

WILL THE BUSINESS BE ABLE TO PAY FOR ITSELF? (CASH FLOW ANALYSIS)

Most buyers have to finance their acquisitions with borrowed money, and they expect the cash flow produced by the company to be adequate to provide the necessary monthly payments. For that reason, no matter what result any valuation method gives, if the cash flow is not adequate to do this, then that price is too high for that buyer.

This is not just a concern for buyers. Sellers should bear this in mind too, because the odds are greatly against finding a huge corporate buyer who is willing to pay cash for a deal without financing it. And there usually has to be some very extraordinary benefit to a particular buyer in order to justify a higher price than cash flow can safely service the debt on.

For the buyer, the first step in determining whether the price passes this test is to prepare a "pro forma*" income statement and balance sheet. This is similar to the "adjusted" income statement discussed in Chapter 3, except that it also anticipates the financial effects of various changes which the buyer feels can realistically be implemented after the acquisition. Preparing this pro forma can be difficult. If lenders or investors will be relying upon it in reviewing the deal, the seller better have solid substantiation to back up every figure. This is no place for estimates or guesswork. Translating improvements into dollars without undue speculation is not easy. It demands a good bit of research. There is a lot at stake and the predictions had better come true.

For this reason, it would be very wise to have the input of accountants who are experienced in working with companies like this. Not only will they be able to flag any faulty assumptions and miscalculations, but if they feel confident that the statement is realistic, they may also offer an opinion letter to that effect, and this is something which carries a great deal of weight with lenders and investors. Their involvement is well worth the cost of their fee.

Preparing a pro forma requires a great deal of consultation with management in order to determine all the places where costs can be cut, where costs will increase, how new efficiencies can be created, and where revenues may be improved. The pro forma should be quite detailed, especially in the various expense categories. All deviations from present performance must be discussed in the notes to the statement. Once again, this is not a time for optimistic speculation. This is a time for conservatism. It may turn out that your pro forma does not differ much from a regular adjusted statement, except that it is for more than one year forward.

Usually you will project the financial results for about ten years into the future. The assumptions and results in each category will differ for each year, and these must all be explained in the notes. Although you must prepare detailed expense statements, the yearly pro formas are usually also summarized, in a column format, so that it is easy to see how they change from year to year in each category.

Once the pro formas have been prepared, refer to Chapter 6 (Discounted Cash Flow Method). To prepare your cash flow analysis, simply follow that method through Step 12, using the figures from your pro forma instead of those from an adjusted income statement. The result is called a Pro Forma Cash Flow Analysis, and each year should conform basically to the format in the "Summary" at the end of Chapter 6. This is not the format used by many accountants, but it will give you the same results. Still have your accountant review it, but don't be surprised if he reformats it. Again, put each year, side by side, in column form.

You will note that this method requires you to assume a purchase price and a loan structure for financing the deal. In most cases, the person conducting a cash flow analysis will have already determined what he is willing to pay for the company, and he just wants to make sure that the company's income will be able to support it. In other cases, you could use a cash flow analysis to help you determine what you might be able to pay for the company. You do this buy "backing into" the purchase price after you know how much cash flow is available for debt payments.

Remember: Do not disregard the need for adequate cash flow safety margins. The risk of any deal is increased greatly when a substantial amount of debt is undertaken by the company. There is always uncertainty in the future, and the risk is especially great where you are depending on predictions for future performance which are different from what has happened in the past. Safety cushions, in each year, of 20% to 50% are the standard requirement.

Remember: Just because the business seems to be able to produce the cash flow needed to service the debt which you anticipate incurring, that does not mean that the company will qualify for a loan of that amount. There must also be adequate security or collateral present in the assets of the company. Only in very unusual circumstances will a lender loan an amount which exceeds the secured loan value of the assets. See Chapter 13 (on secured loan value) in order to help you figure out how much can actually be borrowed.

CHAPTER 16

GLOSSARY

To avoid interrupting each step in the manual with long explanations of the financial terms used, each has been defined separately in this chapter. When they first occur in the text of a chapter, they are marked with an asterisk (*).

We have sought to provide an explanation of each concept only as it relates to the process of valuation. These are not necessarily the most complete or technically correct definitions.

Accounts Payable - A type of debt incurred by a business. Generally encompasses all amounts owed to others for goods and services received on credit. All of the normal unpaid bills of a company. Also referred to as "payables" or "trade payables".

Accounts Receivable - The opposite of accounts payable - these are the bills a company sends to its customers for goods and services sold to them on credit. Also called "receivables" for short.

Receivables can be purchased - that is, you purchase the right to receive the money owed on them and you inherit the place of the original creditor. However, you should not usually pay face value for them. The price should be reduced below book value*
or face value to exclude any probable bad debts among them. These would include receivables from customers who have not paid reliably in the past, and anything which is late or otherwise not being paid according to the agreed upon payment terms. Those remaining should then be reduced in value in order to account for the cost of collecting them, and also by an amount which would give the purchaser a reasonable return on the investment in them. A good analogy is buying a savings bond, which you purchase at a cost lower than face value, so that you have a built-in return which compensates you for your investment.

Agings - Data which shows the amount of accounts payable* or accounts receivable* of a company, and how much time has elapsed since they were billed. For instance, the receivables agings of a company might be shown as the total dollar amount of outstanding, u_npaid bills sent to customers, categorized in increments of 30 days. For example, the following might be the receivables agings for a company which grants "30 day terms" to its customers (bills sent out are due in 30 days):

$600,000 - 15 days or less (have elapsed
         since the bills were sent out)
$500,000 - 16 to 30 days old
$ 50,000 - 31 to 60 days old (past due)
$ 5,000 - 61 to 90 days old (past due)
$ 500 - over 90 days old (past due)

The longer past due they are, the more remote the possibility of ever getting paid. Lenders who look to receivables as security for loans will not generally grant any collateral value for accounts which are past due, unless they are personally guaranteed by the seller or some other party.

Agings generally include an explanation of the company's payment terms, so that the person examining them knows what amounts are within terms, what are past due, and what should probably be viewed as bad debt. Some customers may be granted special payment terms, so not everything which is older than the normal due date is necessarily past due.

Often customers are given a discount if they pay early. That is usually the only reason bills are ever paid before 15 days. For instance, the terms for a receivables policy offering a two percent discount if bills normally due in 30 days are paid by the fifteenth day is expressed as "2% 15, net 30".

Allocation of Purchase Price - This term arises with respect to an acquisition which takes the form of a sale of assets (an "asset deal"). It refers to the process of divvying up the company's purchase price among the various assets purchased, in order to show what each one supposedly cost the purchaser. The purchase price allocation may be hotly negotiated between a buyer and seller since, for tax purposes, both must use the same figures. Therefore, the allocation is usually agreed upon in advance and included in the purchase agreement for the company.

The allocation determines the amount of profit or loss realized by the seller on each asset involved in the sale. The amount of profit or loss on the sale of an asset generally equals its allocated price, minus its "tax basis" (its original cost, plus any amounts spent since then to improve it, minus all depreciation taken on it to date for tax reasons), and minus any "recapture*" of accellerated depreciation or investment tax credits, if applicable.

The allocation also determines what the buyer's starting tax basis (cost) will be for each asset. This is the amount which he can depreciate for tax purposes. Since some assets can be depreciated faster than others, and some can not be depreciated at all, buyers naturally want an allocation which gives them the most advantageous depreciation schedule. They want to minimize or eliminate allocation to non-depreciable assets such as goodwill*.

The seller, on the other hand, is concerned that the allocation is one which results in the smallest possible amount of the purchase price being seen as taxable profit. Generally speaking, taxable profit equals sale proceeds, minus the tax basis of the assets purchased. The seller also wants to see that as much as possible of the taxable profit is attributed to the sale of "capital assets" so that it is considered "capital gain" instead of ordinary income. Then it is taxed at the lower capital gain rate instead of the higher rate for ordinary income.

The tax authorities, on the other hand, feel that the allocation should follow the same proportions which the true economic worth of each asset bears to the total economic value of the all of the assets. They want to discourage allocations which have no relation to economic reality and which are devised solely to decrease the taxes paid by the parties. This means that if the inventory has a market value of $1,000,000, and the total market value of all of the assets purchased is $3,000,000, then one-third of the actual purchase price should be allocated to inventory. If the purchase price is $1,500,000, then $500,000 should be allocated to inventory in this case.

See Step 3 of Chapter 6 for some additional discussion on allocation of purchase price.

Amortization -
  1- The repayment of a loan in periodic installments, instead of in a lump sum. Term loans are amortized by monthly payments for a definite term, at the expiration of which the entire indebtedness has been repaid.
  2- A synonym for depreciation*. The term is sometimes used, for accounting or tax purposes, to refer to the depreciation of intangible assets*.

Assets - Everything the company owns and which has a monetary value. Includes cash, accounts receivable*, inventory or merchandise held for sale, supplies, equipment, buildings, and land. Assets may also include such intangible things as rights which are granted by a patent or copyright. (See "intangible assets", below in this heading).

The balance sheet generally classifies assets into current assets, long-term investments (stocks, bonds, promissory notes for amounts owed to the company, etc.), plant & equipment (known as "fixed assets"), and intangible assets.

Current Assets are those items which are expected to be turned into cash, sold, or consumed within one year. They would include cash itself, accounts receivable and notes receivable which are to be collected within one year, bank deposits, merchandise or inventory (which is expected to be sold within one year), prepaid insurance and the like (which will be consumed), and supplies (which will be consumed).

Such things as prepaid insurance, office supplies, and prepaid taxes are a sub-category of current assets known as "pre-paid expenses". They are purchased for use in the business and will be consumed within a relatively short period of time. Then they become "expenses", but until consumed they are classified as current assets. They are seldom a major item on the balance sheet.

Quick Assets are those assets which can be quickly turned into cash. They generally include cash, accounts receivable, and marketable securities. This is not a category which appears on the balance sheet because it can include both current
assets and long-term investments.

Fixed Assets include land, building, plant and machinery, vehicles, furnishings and fixtures. These are long-lived assets held for use in the production or sale of products and services. Fixed assets, with the exception of land, have a definite value which diminishes gradually over a period of time as they wear out. Since they are consumed over a period which is longer than one year, the IRS does not generally permit their cost to be completely written off (deducted from income) as an expense in the year in which they are purchased.

Usually any asset with a useful life of more than one year is categorized as a fixed asset and depreciated, rather than categorized as an "expense" and expensed. On the balance sheet, the values shown for these fixed assets is their original cost, minus the "depreciation" deducted on them to date. Fixed assets must occasionally be repaired, reconditioned, or improved. In such cases, the cost of doing so is generally added to their original cost (their "tax basis") and depreciated, rather than expensed. The "adjusted basis" of an asset is its original cost, plus the cost of improvements, minus depreciation taken to date.

<u>Intangible Assets</u> are assets having no physical nature. They have no intrinsic value. Instead, their value lies in the rights, savings, or increased income which they represent to their owner. They include such things as goodwill*, patents, copyrights, leasehold improvements, leaseholds, and trademarks. See Chapter 9 for a discussion of intangibles and their value. Since even intangible assets have limited useful lives, when they show up on the balance sheet, their cost is generally depreciated over a period of time. Depreciation of intangibles is often referred to as "amortization". Improvements to leased property are treated as intangibles and are amortized, since they benefit the tenant who put them there, but they become part of the property and revert to the ownership of the landlord at the end of the lease. Notes and accounts receivable are also intangible in nature, but these show up on the balance sheet as current assets. The rights granted under a lease (a "leasehold") are not listed as an asset unless the lease terms require the payment of the rent for an entire year or more in advance, in which case the rent payment may be listed as a leasehold intangible asset instead of a prepaid expense. Normally, rent is paid on a monthly basis and written off as a current expense.

<u>Securable Assets</u> are those assets which lenders will accept as collateral for a loan. Normal-

ly, they are limited to accounts receivable, inventory, land & building, and machinery & equipment. This is not an asset category which appears on the balance sheet, just a way of referring to potential collateral for a loan.

Book Value -
    1- Usually refers to the value of the company's assets, as it is listed on the balance sheet. This figure is the original cost of the asset, less accumulated depreciation. Book value is usually less than actual market value.
    2- The term is also sometimes used to refer to the Net Worth of the company. "Net Worth" is equal to Total Assets minus Total Liabilities, using the figures from the company's balance sheet. See Chapter 10 for a full explanation of this concept.

Capitalization -
    1- The total amount of debt and cash (equity) from which a firm is created. The total investment of the owners in a business.
    2- The process of recording expenditures as long-term assets, which are then depreciated*, instead of as "expenses", which are written off entirely in one year. Such an expense is said to be "capitalized".
    3- "Capitalization of Earnings" - Calculating the present worth of the projected future earnings of a business. See "Discount Rate" for a detailed explanation.

Capital Expenditures - Generally refers to the company's annual investment in new equipment, machinery, real estate, and similar assets of a permanent or fixed nature.

Capital Improvements - Basically the same as Capital Expenditures, but generally refers specifically to sums spent on improvements to a fixed asset already owned, such as real estate.

Cash Flow (Net Cash Flow) - Not the same as "net income" on the company's income statement. Cash flow refers to the actual net inflow and outflow of cash. Since net income on the income statement is a figure which has had certain "expenses" deducted from it which have not necessarily been paid out in cash in the current year (such as depreciation), it is actually less than the true amount of cash the company had available to pay out.

A true cash flow statement will show the cash balance remaining from the previous year, plus the sources of cash and their incoming amounts during the present year, minus uses (outgo) of cash during the year - and end with the new year-end cash balance. A short-cut commonly used to estimate cash flow is to add the depreciation expense back to "net income after tax". The resulting figure shows approximately how much cash is available for further capital expenditures, dividend payments, debt payments, and so on.

Closely-Held - Refers to a corporation whose stock is owned or controlled by a very small group of shareholders.

The term is generally used to refer to a corporation whose stock is publicly registered (with the government agencies which regulate securities) so that it can be publicly traded. However, the closely-held nature of the stock, and the fact that it is rarely traded, makes the company more like a privately-held corporation than it is like a large public corporation. When the stock of a publicly registered company is widely held and actively traded, its value is subject to a number of market influences which do not usually affect a privately-held company's stock. For this reason, closely-held public companies are often valued by the same methods as privately-held companies.

Common Stock - (See "Preferred Stock")

Correlation (of valuation results) - The process of comparing the different results obtained from various valuation methods, and then determining which figures to accord more weight to in arriving at a final result. See Chapter 14.

Current Assets - (See "Assets")

Current Liabilities - Current liabilities are debts or obligations which must be paid within a short time, usually one year, and whose payment will require the use of current assets*. They usually include accounts payable*, notes payable*, wages payable, taxes payable, interest payable, and so on. Also included are "unearned revenues", which are amounts received for goods or services to be delivered at a future time. These are liabilities because they represent an obligation to deliver something at a future date.
 Obligations which are not current liabilities are called long-term debts. These are liabilities which are not due and payable for a comparatively long period, usually more than one year, and they include mortgages and notes payable due more than a year after the balance sheet date.

Debt Service - The annual amount of loan payments, including both principal and interest, which are required to amortize* (pay off in installments) a loan. May include other fees, such as insurance, points*, and other charges required by the lender.

Depreciation - The reduction in the value of an asset over time through wear and tear. An allowance for the depreciation of a company's assets is always made before the calculation of profit or net income on the grounds that the gradual consumption of these "capital assets" is one of the costs of earning the revenues of the business. In effect, the purchase cost of an asset is spread out and deducted over several years, rather than expensed* completely in the year of purchase.
 The only assets that are generally "depreciated", instead of expensed, are those which IRS says can not be completely deducted in the year of purchase. These generally include any asset which lasts more than 12 months. IRS reasons that since they last more than

a year, they are not fully consumed in that first year, so to that extent it is not yet an "expense" to the business. Most businesses, however, given the option, would probably rather deduct it in full in the year of purchase. One major reason is because they have shelled out the money for it in today's dollars, yet through depreciation they get their deduction for it in a mixture of less valuable future dollars.

Depreciation is considered a "non-cash expense". That is, it is real, in the sense that there is a legitimate loss of value in the asset, but no additional funds have been paid out by the company for this expense over and above its initial cost.

Depreciation, for financial statement purposes, requires an estimate of the useful life of the asset, and of its salvage (scrap) value at end of the period. The difference between its cost and its salvage value is divided by the number of years of useful life, and the resulting amount is what is allowed as a depreciation deduction each year. This is called the "straight line method".

There are also "accelerated" methods of depreciation which use various formulas and allow a faster write-off of the cost of the asset. They usually allow greater deduction in the earlier years of the useful life than in the later years. Depreciation for tax return purposes can be different than that used for financial statements because of the write-off periods which are dictated by the IRS for certain types of assets.

It should be noted that obsolescence is different from depreciation, in that the former is an unforeseen change in the value of an asset due to technological or economic reasons. If an asset becomes obsolete, its undepreciated value is usually written off completely in the year of replacement. Where there is high risk of obsolescence, an asset can sometimes be depreciated over a shorter period of time.

Not all assets used in a business or held for the production of income are depreciable under the tax code. Land and goodwill are examples of assets for which depreciation has traditionally not been allowed in order to reduce taxes.

See Step 3 of Chapter 6 for some additional discussion of depreciation.

<u>Discount Rate</u> - The most common use of this term refers to the interest rate charged by the Federal Reserve in loans made to its member banks. However, we use the term in valuation to refer to the interest rate which is used to calculate the present value* of a sum of money to be received in the future. The "discount rate" is thus converted into one of two forms, each of which has a different application:

1- <u>Capitalization Rate</u>* - This is a single percentage rate used to convert a <u>series</u> of payments or earnings into a <u>single</u> present value in one step. A discount rate is called a "capitalization rate" when it is used in this way. Accordingly, "capitalization of earnings" is the process of estimating the economic worth of a company by computing the present value of <u>average annual</u> net income expected during the future. To do this, first estimate what the average annual net income will be in future years, and then <u>divide</u> this figure by the appropriate percentage rate (capitalization rate).

For example, say you are trying to establish the present value of a certain investment which is expected to yield an annual return of $15,000, and which has a risk factor which equates to other investments with annual returns of 10%. You want to know the present value of the stream of income which will be received from this investment. The projected average annual income of $15,000, divided by a rate of 10 percent, gives the present value of that investment as $150,000. Here the income of $15,000 has been "capitalized" at a capitalization rate of 10%.

Two practical difficulties are encountered when trying to use the Capitalization of Earnings technique. First is the problem of reliably estimating the future flow of net income on an average annual basis. The other problem is determining the correct interest rate at which to capitalize this net income. The rate selected must reflect a number of considerations. Since the rate of return from an investment is always commensurate with the degree of risk involved with it, that risk must be accurately assessed. One consideration bearing on risk is the reliability of the earnings estimate. Another thing to take into consideration is the rate of return generally expected on investments that would seem to offer comparable risk. While there is no way to be absolutely certain in the determination of an appropriate rate of capitalization, one must be as accurate as possible. Because this determination is so crucial, capitalization of income is a useful device only where you are familiar enough with the particular business to accurately appraise its risk level.

In review - a capitalization rate is a form of discount rate which is used to convert a stream of annual incomes, which will be received <u>indefinitely</u> into the future, into a single present value. This is done by dividing the average expected annual income by the capitalization rate.

2- <u>Discount factor</u> - A "discount factor" is a form of discount rate which is used to determine the present value* of a right to receive a <u>single</u> payment at a <u>specified time</u> in the future. Present value is determined by simply <u>multiplying</u> the amount to be received by the discount factor (not dividing it).

The discount factor is the reciprocal of one, plus the discount rate, or $(1 + i)^{-n}$. Here, "i" equals the estimated rate of interest which would probably otherwise be earned on the money during the period before its actual receipt, and "n" refers to the number of periods until the expected receipt.

For example, if the discount rate is 10 percent per period, the discount factor for three periods is $(1.10)^{-3} = 0.75131$. If the amount to be received in three years is $10,000, then the right to receive that amount has a present value today of $10,000 X 0.75131 = $7,513.10. In this form, the discount rate represents the alternative return sacrificed by the investor because he has committed his funds to the investment being valued.

You don't actually have to use the formula above to calculate the factor, since tables showing the discount

factors at various rates are readily available (see the Appendix), and since many financial calculators also perform this function with ease.
See "present value" also.

Earnings - The terms "profit", "net operating profit", "net operating income", "net income", and "net profit" are often used synonymously. But they may be viewed as technically having slightly different meanings. The common thread between them is that they all refer to the income of the business from sales of goods or services, after deducting the expenses of producing that income. For accounting purposes, however, the terms are used differently. Compare the following:

Gross Profit: Total sales revenue, minus the "cost of goods sold" (the cost of raw materials, direct labor, freight, and factory overhead costs - including depreciation- used in the production of the goods sold).

Operating Income or Operating Profit: Gross Profit, minus "operating expenses". Operating expenses are selling expenses, delivery expenses, administrative expenses, and other general expenses (office salaries, office supplies, office expense, bad debt expense, depreciation on office equipment, etc.)

Net Income or Net Profit: Operating Profit, minus taxes, interest paid on mortgage loans, and other remaining financial expenses.

"Earnings" generally refers to Net Income (also known as Net Profit). For an illustrative explanation of all of these terms, see the definition for "Income Statement".

Expense (to Expense) (verb) - A term which refers to the practice of deducting a cost or expense entirely in the year in which it is incurred, rather than depreciating it (which spreads the deduction out over several years). In this case, it is said to be "expensed". Sometimes a business can elect to write off an expense in one year which would normally be depreciated. See "Assets", under the discussion for Fixed Assets.

Goodwill - That portion of the value of a company which is in excess of the value of its assets. It refers to any extraordinary "ongoing-business value" which accompanies those assets. Methods of calculating the value of goodwill vary, but most generally boil it down to:
> the capitalized* value . . .
> of the amount of earnings produced by the
> > business . . .
> which are in excess of the cost of financing
> > the purchase of that business.

It would seem that goodwill has a different meaning in practice than it does in theory, because it is rather difficult sometimes to get any value at all accorded to what seem to be goodwill factors in a business. Simply having a collection of assets which is assembled in the form of an ongoing business does not automatically mean there is goodwill value in the eyes of most analysts.

Most businesses, even poorly operated ones, possess customer accounts, ongoing patronage, and some sort of established business reputation, but that does not in itself seem to be enough to give them goodwill value. In the practice of valuation, goodwill exists only in the situation where the expected earnings of the business are greater than normal for its industry. It refers to a special competitive edge held by that firm which sets it apart from the others, and which can reasonably be expected to continue in the future.

For illustrations of the valuation of goodwill, see Chapter 9, Chapter 11, and Step 7 of Chapter 8.

Income Statement - (Also known as a "Profit and Loss Statement", or "P&L") A statement of annual revenue and expenses which shows whether the company earned a profit ("net income").

On the following page is the usual format of an Income Statement for a manufacturing company. Following that are detailed breakdowns of certain items included on the Income Statement which are calculated separately.

Income Statement
Summary Form

Gross Sales
    Less: Sales returns and allowances
    Less: Cash discounts

= Net Sales
    Less: Cost of Goods Sold[1] (detailed breakdown below)

= Gross Profit
    Less: Operating Expenses[3] (detailed breakdown below)

= Operating Income (or Operating Profit)
    Less: Interest and other financial expenses

= Net Income before Taxes
    Less: Income Taxes

= Net Income

Detailed Breakdowns

[1]Cost of Goods Sold:

    Finished Goods Inventory at Beginning of Year
+ Cost of Goods Manufactured[2] (detailed breakdown below)
- Finished Goods Inventory at End of Year

= Cost of Goods Sold

(continued)

[2]Cost of Goods Manufactured:

      Raw Materials used during year (beginning inventory, plus purchases, minus ending inventory)
- \+ Direct Manufacturing Labor Costs (includes wages, Workman's Compensation, and Payroll expenses)
- \+ Factory Overhead Costs:
  - supervision
  - power
  - repairs and maintenance
  - factory supplies
  - factory insurance
  - depreciation on machinery & equipment
  - depreciation on building used for manufacturing
  - taxes on property used for mnfg.
  - other misc. labor ("indirect labor")
- \+ Beginning "Work-in-Process" Inventory
- − End of Year "Work-in-Process" Inventory

= Cost of Goods Manufactured

[3]Operating Expenses:

    Selling Expenses:
- Sales salaries and commissions
- Advertising and promotion expense
- Travel and entertainment expense
- Delivery expenses (not prev. deducted)
- Sales supplies and shipping supplies
- Insurance or Delivery expense
- Bad debts expense
- Credit and collection
- Depreciation expense for delivery equipment

\+ Administrative Expenses:
- Salaries and wages - executive & clerical
- Travel and entertainment

      Telephone
      Postage, stationary, supplies
      Dues and publications
      Depreciation on office equipment
      Rental expense for office equipment
      Miscellaneous Administrative expenses

+ General Expenses:
      Group insurance and other employee benefits
      General insurance
      Legal and accounting expense
      Payroll taxes (for non-manufacturing employees)
      Other real estate taxes
      Workmans Compensation expense (for non manufacturing personnel)
      Liability insurance
      Miscellaneous General Expense

= Total Operating Expense

Note: The Income Statement includes as expenses certain "non-cash expenses" (amounts deducted on the income statement as expenses for which no cash may actually have been paid out in the current year - such as depreciation). For this reason Net Income is not the same as Net Cash Flow*. See the separate definition for "Cash Flow".

Intangible Assets - (See "Assets")

Leasehold Improvements - Physical improvements of a permanent nature made to leased property by its tenant. The cost of these improvements is generally depreciated* by the tenant over the term of the lease, or over the life of the improvements, whichever is shorter. Ownership of the improvements reverts to the landlord at the end of the lease term, even thought they have been paid for by the tenant. These may include "fixtures" - which are items of property which could be removed from the premises, but since they are attached in a more permanent fashion, the lease generally provides that, once attached, they stay with the property.

Leveraged Buyout - Generally refers to an acquisition which is financed with very little cash ("equity") and a lot of debt. In an "LBO", the normal cash investment of 20% to 30% may be cut back to 10% or less, depending on the circumstances. There are two conditions in particular which lenders require before agreeing to finance such a highly leveraged deal:

1- The company must possess a large base of securable assets, available as collateral for the loan.

2- The company must have stable, healthy cash flow* adequate to service the loan payments with a large margin left over for safety.

The correct purchase price is very important in such deals, for it must be limited to an amount which does not result in annual loan payments exceeding the cash flow conservatively expected, along with a safety cushion of 30% to 50%. This cushion assures the lenders that, despite possible fluctuations in performance, the company will still be able to safely meet its obligations.

Due to the unusually high debt service demands on the company, these loan situations are much riskier than normal for the lender, so amounts in excess of the secured loan value of the collateral assets generally can not be borrowed. (See Chapter 13 on "Secured Loan Value") However, the combination of the right purchase price, a large securable asset base, and good net cash flow makes some very significant acquisitions possible for buyers who have relatively little cash available to invest in a company.

LIFO Inventory Accounting Method - ("Last in, first out"). Under this method of inventory accounting, it is assumed that the last inventory purchased is the first inventory used in producing the goods sold during the current period. In other words, the cost of the last materials purchased is the raw materials or inventory expense which you offset sales with in order to determine net income for the latest period.

The theory behind LIFO is that a sale depletes inventory and necessitates the replacement of goods. Therefore, those replacement costs should be matched with the sales which induced them. Since the higher cost of more recent materials purchases are used to offset sales income, the taxable net profit will be less for the business than if it was assumed that goods purchased earlier at a lower cost are used up first.

This is an attractive tax break for most businesses when inventory costs are rising. Old inventory purchased at lower prices of the past remains on the books at those prices, even though its true value may be significantly higher, or even though it may actually have long been used up. Therefore, the book value of inventory accounted for under the LIFO method may be considerably understated.

Other inventory accounting methods include:

<u>FIFO</u> - Where it is assumed that the oldest merchandise or materials are used up or sold first. This matches old, lower costs with new sales.

<u>Weighted Average</u> - Smooths out inventory cost fluctuations by using a weighted average of past inventory purchase costs.

<u>Specific Invoice Price</u> - When it is possible to identify each item in an inventory with a specific materials purchase invoice, this method may be used to assign those specific costs to the inventory and to the goods sold. It exactly matches costs and revenues. Most businesses cannot use this method.

<u>Liquidation Value</u> - Refers to the amount of money which is likely to be received from the sale of the individual assets of a business, when that business is terminated and its assets are sold piecemeal. Liquida-

tion implies that the assets are being sold under hasty or forced circumstances, at an auction, so that the price is likely to be somewhat less than market value*.

The liquidation value of an entire company is the total of the liquidation values of all of its saleable assets, minus the company's liabilities, minus the costs of liquidating those assets (brokerage and auction commissions, sales taxes, transfer taxes, accounting fees, attorneys fees, appraisal fees, and so on). See Chapter 9 for a complete explanation of liquidation value of a company.

Liquidation is often initiated by the company's creditors due to financial insolvency. Lenders and investors are interested in liquidation value because if a business fails after acquisition, they will be forced to foreclose as creditors, and they want to make sure that all of the money owed to them can be repaid from an auction sale of the assets. They don't want to be bothered with trying to get top dollar price for the assets in order to get all of their money back. They insist that they are able to be repaid through the least inconvenient means possible: a quick auction sale. Even then, having to go through a foreclosure and liquidation is a procedural nightmare for them.

Buyers are interested in liquidation value because they want to know that they can retrieve their own cash investment in the company after the other creditors ahead of them have been repaid. They also want to make sure that those other creditors are repaid in full so that there are no amounts left unpaid for which they might be held personally liable.

Sellers are interested in liquidation value because that usually represents the minimum possible value of their company - the rock bottom price they can receive.

See Chapter 9 for information on determining liquidation value.

<u>Liquidity</u> - The relative quickness and ease with which an asset can be sold or converted to cash.

<u>Market Value</u> (or "Fair Market Value") - Refers to that price which a seller is likely to receive

from the sale of an asset, as the result of a process of arm's length negotiation between a willing buyer and seller, neither being under any compulsion to act, and both having reasonable knowledge of all relevant facts. It does not refer to the best price that could be obtained in the current market. Market value appraisals always estimate value as of a specific date.

Net Profit - (See "Earnings" and "Income Statement")

Net Sales - The total amount of revenues received by a business from the sale of goods and services ("gross sales"), less sales returns and allowances, and cash discounts to customers. (See "Income Statement")

Multiple - Generally refers to a number which is multiplied times sales or income to produce an estimate of value for the business. Used as a rough gauge in rule-of-thumb valuation methods. The multiple generally corresponds to a capitalization rate* - the annual rate of return which would reasonably be expected by an investor in such a transaction, chosen to provide adequate compensation for the level of risk undertaken. For example, a 12% capitalization rate equates with a multiple of 8.3 (1 divided by 12%). This is because when you "capitalize" a figure by 12%, you divide that figure by 12%. That is the same thing as multiplying it by 1 divided by .12 .

For more on the use of multiples in valuation, see Chapter 12 (the section on the Price/Earnings Ratio Method, and the section on Rule-of-Thumb Pricing Methods), and the introduction to Chapter 7.

Non-Amortizing - (See "Amortize")

Notes Payable - Promissory notes, executed by the company, which evidence a debt owed to another. On the balance sheet, they can be classified as either Long-Term Liabilities (if not due and payable for more than a year) or Current Liabilities (if they must be paid within one year).

Notes Receivable - Promissory notes executed by a party owing a sum of money to the company. On the balance sheet, these may be classified as either Long-Term Notes Receivable (if they are not expected to be repaid within one year) or Current Assets (if they are expected to be realized in cash within 12 months).

Note that notes receivable should be valued according to the same theory as accounts receivable*: they should be reduced in value to reflect any probable bad debts, and they should then be discounted in order to give the buyer a reasonable return on his investment in them, and to compensate him for the cost of maintaining and collecting them. (See "Accounts Receivable")

Note that long-term notes receivable from the owners of a company may be on the books without the intention that they will ever be repaid. If such is the case, these should obviously be assigned no value. This a technique sometimes used so that owners can take money out of the business tax-free, and the obligation is later written off as a bad debt.

Operating Profit - (See "Income Statement", and "Earnings")

Percentage Operating Profit - On an income statement, items of income and expense are often expressed not only in dollars, but also as a percentage of net sales. In other words, if Operating Income is $600,000, and Net Sales are $4,000,000, then Percentage Operating Income is 600,000/4,000,000 = 15%. So, if it could be assumed that the same level of profitability would continue into the next year, but next year's net sales are forecast at $5,500,000, then the operating profit for next year will be forecast at $5,500,000 X .15 = $825,000, using the "percentage operating profit".

Perks or Perquisites - Refers to incidental benefits which flow to an employee, beyond the normal salary or compensation received. These may take the form of unusual favors, or consideration, or status, or the privilege to enjoy certain amenities. They also include the receipt of "fringe benefits" which relieve expenses which would otherwise have to be paid for by the recipient out of his own pocket.

We are concerned mostly with the latter in valuation, for these are items which involve an ascertainable expense to the company which should be added back into income when adjusting a company's income statement, in order to reflect a more normal state of affairs. Perquisites are often personal expenses taken as business expenses. They might include such things as automobiles, large travel and entertainment allowances, country club dues, vacation homes. life insurance, or higher than normal salaries.

Points - A charge made to a borrower by a lender at the time the funds are transferred. While usually labeled as a charge for certain services involved with originating the loan, points are generally just a way for the lender to arrange a higher amount of interest from a borrower than might normally be allowed by law or convention. A "point" is one-percent of the loan amount.

Preferred Stock - (To be distinguished from Common Stock) A separate variety (class) of stock of a corporation which is accorded, by the company's charter or by-laws, a priority with respect to the payment of dividends and with respect to distributions made upon liquidation of the company. The specific rights attached to preferred stock are spelled out in detail in the articles of incorporation (charter), and these may be customized to fit the needs and desires of the company and of the investors.

Generally, holders of the preferred stock are entitled to receive a fixed dividend amount, which is paid out of the surplus earnings of the corporation. The dividend may generally not exceed the amount stated on the stock certificate, but it must be paid before any dividend is paid to the holders of the common stock. The fixed dividend may be "cumulative" or "noncumulative". If cumulative, dividends not paid in any one year accumulate and carry into succeeding years as a charge against earnings which must be paid in full before any common stock dividend is paid. If dividends are non-cumulative, they do not accumulate from year to year and the right to receive the dividend for any given year is extinguished by the company's failure to earn and formally declare the dividend in that year.

There may be different types of preferred stock issued by the same corporation, each with different benefits and priorities, as defined in the charter or by-laws of the corporation. Preferred stock is non-voting, and it is typically entitled to a vote only when its dividends have been in arrears for a stated period. Although preferred stock obviously has some attributes of debt, it does not have a fixed maturity date. Instead, it usually provides for redemption or "call" by the board of directors, at which time the corporation buys it back.

<u>Common Stock</u> is stock which entitles its holders to an equal pro rata division of surplus profits or net earnings, without any preference or priority among common stockholders. Such dividends are declared at the discretion of the board of directors. Upon liquidation of the company or any of its assets, common stockholders share evenly in a division of the proceeds, after any preferred stockholders have been paid.

It is important to note that dividends are paid out of the <u>after</u>-tax net income of the corporation and are not a deductible expense of the company on its tax return. On the other hand, the income paid to the holder of a debt-type financing instrument is classified as "interest". Interest on an indebtedness is a deductible expense which is paid out of the <u>before</u> tax earnings. Therefore, if possible, it is generally regarded as preferable for a comp any to finance itself through debt or borrowing rather than through stock offerings, because the cost to the company of paying the investor a return of exactly the same amount is so much greater when it is in the form of a stock dividend. (Not to mention the fact that additional stock dilutes the ownership interests of the existing stockholders.)

Pre-Paid Expenses - (See "Assets", under the paragraph on "Current Assets")

Present Value - The value today of something which will be received in the future. Present value calculation is based on the premise that a dollar received today is worth more than a dollar received tomorrow. Disregarding the effects of inflation, this is because, by not having that dollar in your possession, investment income from the money is lost in the meantime.

Therefore, if a business makes an investment today that will return $1 a year from now, that $1 has a "present value" which is somewhat less than $1. How much less depends upon how much the business expects to earn on its investments. If it expects to earn a 10% annual return, the expectation of receiving $1 a year from now has a present value of $0.909. $0.909 invested today at 10% annual interest will accumulate to a total value of $1 in one year. In this situation, the present value of one dollar is $0.909.

See "Discount Rate" for additional information on the topic of present value, and directions on how to use the present value tables located in the Appendix to find the present value of a sum to be received in the future. Also see the comment in Step 13 of Chapter 6.

In the valuation of a business, present value calculation is used because the buyer is viewed as purchasing future earnings. Those earnings must be discounted in order to arrive at the present value of the business. The methods outlined in this manual are fairly straightforward in explaining how present value enters into each of them. The remainder of this heading discusses a slightly more involved use of present value, and is wholly optional, but reading it may help increase your understanding of the concept.

In any investment, a rate of return is demanded which justifies the risk to the investor. To determine whether an investment will earn the required return, the anticipated annual income from the investment is discounted at that rate in order to see if it adds up to the total expected over the term of the investment.

For example, a company has an opportunity to invest

$20,000 in a project, the risk of which justifies a 12% compound return. The investment will return an estimated $10,000 at the end of the first year, $9,000 at the end of the second year, $8,000 at the end of the third year, and nothing thereafter. Will the project return the original investment, plus the 12% demanded?
The following calculations show that it will, plus something extra.

Year	Expected Return	Present Value of $1 at 12% (discount factor)	Present Val. of Expected Returns
1	$10,000	0.893	$8,930
2	$ 9,000	0.797	$7,173
3	$ 8,000	0.712	$5,696

Total present value of the returns $21,799
Minus: Original investment   - $20,000

Excess over the 12% return demanded $ 1,799

If the total return, when discounted to present value at the anticipated rate of return, is at least equal to the amount originally invested, then that required return has been earned.

Privately-Held - A corporation which does not offer its stock for investment to the public at large. The stock of privately-held companies is generally held by its founders and managers, and possibly by a very small group of outside investors.

Stock of companies which is traded on the public stock exchanges or offered to the public in general must be registered with the Securities Exchange Commission. It is subject to a great deal of restrictive regulation, and the companies issuing such stock are required to comply with very involved requirements for disclosure of company information, notice to shareholders on matters affecting the value and risk of the stock, shareholder meetings, elections of board members, and so on.   Privately-held companies are exempt from all of this.

The acquisition of a publicly-held company can be quite involved from a procedural standpoint. It usually involves a "tender offer" - or individually addressed offer to each shareholder for the purchase of his stock, which must comply with certain very explicit SEC requirements. The tender offer is usually either indorsed by the board of directors, or not indorsed, and this often determines the success of the acquisition. Usually a specified minimum number of shares must accept before the offer is valid. Acquisitions of non-public corporations do not have to comply with this regulation, although there may be some other, less involved SEC (or state corporation commission) requirements to deal with.

NOTE: Because their value is affected by stock market influences which privately-held companies are not subject to, publicly-held companies are generally valued by different methods than those described in this book. The only exception might be when their stock is actually held by a very small number of people, and rarely traded. Consult your accountant or investment banker in every case.

Profit - (See "Earnings")

Pro Forma - This term generally refers to a projected financial statement for a future year. A pro forma statement is entirely speculative. It does not reflect results which the present state of affairs at the company would produce. Instead, it shows what the results for a new venture might be, or what effect certain changes in an existing venture might have on performance, including sales.

It differs from an "adjusted financial statement" (Chapter 3) in that the latter is based only on what the company has already historically shown it can accomplish. On an adjusted statement, the only difference from present performance involves changes in accounting methods, increased expenses which would be incurred under more realistic post-acquisition circumstances, and the elimination of any obviously excessive expenses or perquisites*. It does not attempt to show increased revenues, or the elimination of any expense for which there is any doubt concerning its continued necessity.

By offering a pro forma, one is saying that they believe that those results can and will be attained. However, to be believable, the document must contain information which supports every figure on it. Still, pro forma results are not anything which can really be substantiated with certainty. For this reason, they should never be the basis for a valuation. Only historic results should be used for valuation, with conservative adjustments at most. Another reason why pro formas should not be used for valuation is that the sellers are supposed to get paid for what they have actually done, not for what the new owner "might" be able to do in the future.

Publicly-Held - (See "Privately-Held")

Recapture - There are circumstances under which the amount of gain you must declare for tax purposes upon the sale of an asset will be increased by the amount of investment tax credits or "accellerated" depreciation claimed in the past with regard to that asset. If such credits or deductions have been taken, then consult an up to date tax guide or tax accountant with regard to recapture. "Recapture" means that the amount deducted on your tax return is considered to have come back into your hands, as taxable income.

Receivables - (See "Accounts Receivable")

Secured Debt - A debt for which collateral has been posted. The lender is given a conditional interest in specific property of the borrower. In the event of the borrower's default on repayment of the loan, the lender has the right to seize possession of the property, or have it sold to obtain repayment of the debt.

If an unsecured debt is defaulted on, the lender must get a legal judgment against the borrower for the amount of the debt, and then take further legal action to levy upon the general assets of the borrower in order to obtain repayment. It is a much more cumbersome process, and there is often no certainty that there will even be sufficient assets there for the sheriff to seize and sell.

If the borrower defaults on both secured and unsecured debts at the same time, those lenders holding security interests in specific property have priority as to that property. The unsecured creditors will only have what is left after the secured creditors have levied upon their security and been repaid. Among secured creditors holding security interests in the same property, generally speaking, those who have recorded their security agreements first as a matter of public record will have first priority.

See Chapter 13 for directions on determining the Secured Loan Value of assets (how much money can be borrowed against them).

(Sub-Chapter) S Corporations - An otherwise normal corporation whose profits are taxed more like a partnership's than a corporation's. It uses different accounting and is taxed differently than the normal corporation. Consult your accountant when dealing with companies organized as S corporations.

According to the rules in effect at the time of this writing, S Corporation status must be elected by unanimous consent of the shareholders. The company pays no corporate tax on its income, but instead the shareholders pay taxes on it themselves (their distributive share) even though such income may not have actually been distributed to them. It is often elected when the investors think that the company is going to sustain net losses.

The important thing to note in valuation is that we always look at each company valued as a normal corporation. Therefore, when you are adjusting the income statements prior to doing your calculations, you must assume that the S Corporation is a normal corporation and deduct what the company would normally pay in corporate income taxes from the company's net income.

Subordinated Debt (or "Junior Debt") - A type of debt or loan whereby the lender agrees to stand behind other lenders with regard to the priority of his claim against the assets of the borrower in the event the borrower defaults on his loans.
Upon default, the creditors of the borrower would take action to levy upon those assets in order to get repaid. The lenders standing first in the priority of their claims are the "senior lenders". Senior lenders may have their loans secured by first priority liens on the specific property of the borrower, or the terms (and earlier recording) of their loan agreements may simply provide that they have first claim against the borrower's assets in general. Normally, the order of claims is determined not only by the terms of the loan agreements, but also by the order in which those security agreements are filed as public notice.

In exchange for taking the increased risk that there will not be sufficient assets left to be fully repaid, the subordinated lender usually requires a higher rate of interest on its loan. It may also demand an "equity sweetener" in the form of common stock, or a right to convert the debt to common stock, or a warrant to buy stock at a certain low price later on.

Tangible Assets - (See "Assets")

Turnaround - Refers to the process of turning a poorly performing business into a successful one. Often used to refer to an acquisition plan which involves the purchase and refinancing of an unprofitable company, followed by a radical restructuring of the way it does business. Turnarounds are viewed as risky and speculative ventures.

Weighted Average - In cases where you want to refer to historic figures from the company's past performance, but they have fluctuated greatly from year to year, a "weighted average" seems to give a better representation of what the company is doing than does a regular average. It assigns progressively more importance to the figures from the most recent years. To calculate a weighted average, take the most recent year's figure and multiply it times five. Add to that the previous years's figure multiplied times four. Add to that the next previous year's figure multiplied by three, the figure from the year before that multiplied by two, and the figure from the year before that multiplied by one. Then add them up and divide the total by 15. The result if your weighted average.

Working Capital - This term refers to the money used by a company to carry on its business. A company can have a building and a collection of equipment, but before it can get anywhere it has to have some cash to run that business and produce its products or services.
This is its working capital. Working capital is not cash which is simply consumed, it just changes form. It is transformed into raw materials and labor, and then into products, and then into accounts receivable and then back into cash (hopefully more cash). From an accounting point of view, the total amount of working capital is the excess of a company's current assets* over its current liabilities*.

Adequate working capital is necessary in order for a business to be able to carry sufficient inventories, meet current debts, take advantage of cash discounts, and extend favorable terms to customers. A company with deficient working capital is in a poor competitive position and its survival chances are normally small.

For the purpose of projecting the working capital needs of the company in a valuation, "Working Capital" can be considered to be the sum of:

> Current Assets* - such as cash, accounts receivable*, inventory, etc. (see your balance sheet for other current assets listed)

(minus) Current Liabilities* - such as accounts payable*.

See Step 10 of Chapter 6 for specific instructions on how to estimate future working capital requirements. When actually planning the working capital needs of a business, always consult your accountant.

APPENDIX: PRESENT VALUE TABLES

Present Value of $1

$$P = F_n(1 + r)^{-n}$$

r = discount rate; n = number of periods until payment; F_n = $1

Periods = n	¼%	½%	¾%	1%	1½%	2%	3%	4%	5%	6%	7%	8%	10%	12%	15%	20%
1	.99751	.99502	.99256	.99010	.98522	.98039	.97087	.96154	.95238	.94340	.93458	.92593	.90909	.89286	.86957	.83333
2	.99502	.99007	.98517	.98030	.97066	.96117	.94260	.92456	.90703	.89000	.87344	.85734	.82645	.79719	.75614	.69444
3	.99254	.98515	.97783	.97059	.95632	.94232	.91514	.88900	.86384	.83962	.81630	.79383	.75131	.71178	.65752	.57870
4	.99006	.98025	.97055	.96098	.94218	.92385	.88849	.85480	.82270	.79209	.76290	.73503	.68301	.63552	.65175	.48225
5	.98759	.97537	.96333	.95147	.92826	.90573	.86261	.82193	.78353	.74726	.71299	.68058	.62092	.56743	.49718	.40188
6	.98513	.97052	.95616	.94205	.91454	.88797	.83748	.79031	.74622	.70496	.66634	.63017	.56447	.50663	.43233	.33490
7	.98267	.96569	.94904	.93272	.90103	.87056	.81309	.75992	.71068	.66506	.62275	.58349	.51316	.45235	.37594	.27908
8	.98022	.96089	.94198	.92348	.88771	.85349	.78941	.73069	.67684	.62741	.58201	.54027	.46651	.40388	.32690	.23257
9	.97778	.95610	.93496	.91434	.87459	.83676	.76642	.70259	.64461	.59190	.54393	.50025	.42410	.36061	.28426	.19381
10	.97534	.95135	.92800	.90529	.86167	.82035	.74409	.67556	.61391	.55839	.50835	.46319	.38554	.32197	.24718	.16151
11	.97291	.94661	.92109	.89632	.84893	.80426	.72242	.64958	.58468	.52679	.47509	.42888	.35049	.28748	.21494	.13459
12	.97048	.94191	.91424	.88745	.83639	.78849	.70138	.62460	.55684	.49697	.44401	.39711	.31863	.25668	.18691	.11216
13	.96806	.93722	.90743	.87866	.82403	.77303	.68095	.60057	.53032	.46884	.41496	.36770	.28966	.22917	.16253	.09346
14	.96565	.93256	.90068	.86996	.81185	.75788	.66112	.57748	.50507	.44230	.38782	.34046	.26333	.20462	.14133	.07789
15	.96324	.92792	.89397	.86135	.79985	.74301	.64186	.55526	.48102	.41727	.36245	.31524	.23939	.18270	.12289	.06491
16	.96084	.92330	.88732	.85282	.78803	.72845	.62317	.53391	.45811	.39365	.33873	.29189	.21763	.16312	.10686	.05409
17	.95844	.91871	.88071	.84438	.77639	.71416	.60502	.51337	.43630	.37136	.31657	.27027	.19784	.14564	.09293	.04507
18	.95605	.91414	.87416	.83602	.76491	.70016	.58739	.49363	.41552	.35034	.29586	.25025	.17986	.13004	.00081	.03756
19	.95367	.90959	.86765	.82774	.75361	.68643	.57029	.47464	.39573	.33051	.27651	.23171	.16351	.11611	.07027	.03130
20	.95129	.90506	.86119	.81954	.74247	.67297	.55368	.45639	.37689	.31180	.25842	.21455	.14864	.10367	.06110	.02608
22	.94655	.89608	.84842	.80340	.72069	.64684	.52189	.42196	.34185	.27751	.22571	.18394	.12285	.08264	.04620	.01811
24	.94184	.88719	.83583	.78757	.69954	.62172	.49193	.39012	.31007	.24698	.19715	.15770	.10153	.06588	.03493	.01258
26	.93714	.87838	.82343	.77205	.67902	.59758	.46369	.36069	.28124	.21981	.17220	.13520	.08391	.05252	.02642	.00874
28	.93248	.86966	.81122	.75684	.65910	.57437	.43708	.33348	.25509	.19563	.15040	.11591	.06934	.04187	.01997	.00607
30	.92783	.86103	.79919	.74192	.63976	.55207	.41199	.30832	.23138	.17411	.13137	.09938	.05731	.03338	.01510	.00421
32	.92321	.85248	.78733	.72730	.62099	.53063	.38834	.28506	.20987	.15496	.11474	.08520	.04736	.02661	.01142	.00293
34	.91861	.84402	.77565	.71297	.60277	.51003	.36604	.26355	.19035	.13791	.10022	.07305	.03914	.02121	.00864	.00203
36	.91403	.83564	.76415	.69892	.58509	.49022	.34503	.24367	.17266	.12274	.08754	.06262	.03235	.01691	.00653	.00141
38	.90948	.82735	.75281	.68515	.56792	.47119	.32523	.22529	.15661	.10924	.07646	.05369	.02673	.01348	.00494	.00098
40	.90495	.81914	.74165	.67165	.55126	.45289	.30656	.20829	.14205	.09722	.06678	.04603	.02209	.01075	.00373	.00068
45	.89372	.79896	.71445	.63905	.51171	.41020	.26444	.17120	.11130	.07265	.04761	.03133	.01372	.00610	.00186	.00027
50	.88263	.77929	.68825	.60804	.47500	.37153	.22811	.14071	.08720	.05429	.03395	.02132	.00852	.00346	.00092	.00011
100	.77904	.60729	.47369	.36971	.22563	.13803	.05203	.01980	.00760	.00295	.00115	.00045	.00007	.00001	.00000	.00000

INDEX

accountant   11-13, 28, 39, 44-45, 62, 65, 72-74, 79-83, 92, 120, 127-128, 130, 169, 173, 175, 182-185, 213-215, 218
accounts payable   30, 32, 81-85, 103, 106, 187-188, 195
    accounts receivable   30, 44, 73-76, 81-83, 101-106, 112, 160, 161, 187-193, 208, 214, 217
accuracy   10, 12, 45, 53, 74, 105, 123, 162, 198
acquisition agreement   153
agings   30, 188, 189
allocation of purchase price   61-62, 72-73, 127-128, 174-175, 189-190
asset appraisal   12, 14, 16, 29, 51, 75, 100-102, 112-114, 158, 162, 206-207
asset value   101, 103-104, 106, 110, 113, 114, 123-126
assets, current   103, 191, 192, 195, 208, 211, 217
attorney   122, 128, 170, 182, 206
auctions   22, 112, 114, 158, 161, 206
auto expense   40, 41, 56, 111, 114, 200, 209
book value   7, 29, 52, 75, 100, 103, 113, 124, 126, 159, 188, 193, 205
calculators   65, 78, 87, 199
capital expenditures   29, 50, 63, 64, 66, 73-74, 79-80, 89, 93, 180-181, 193-194
capitalization   32, 51-52, 91-97, 105-108, 113-118, 120, 125, 128-130, 156-157, 193, 197-198, 200, 207
cash flow   9, 15, 20, 44, 49-50, 55-57, 62-68, 72-74, 77-78, 80, 85-93, 113, 157-158, 164, 170, 173-174, 176, 182-186, 194, 203-204
closely-held corp.   52, 152, 154, 194
common stock   94, 194, 210, 216
competition   31, 105, 119, 180-182
    covenant against   119, 179
contracts   7, 32, 119-122, 150, 169, 178
debt service   50, 57, 62-66, 80, 85-86, 89, 93, 158, 164, 195, 204
depreciation   19, 29, 38, 43-44, 60-63, 66, 71-74, 80, 89, 93-94, 96, 100, 102, 108, 112, 124-127, 162, 173-176, 189, 190-199, 202-203, 214
discount rate   87, 117, 119, 122, 193, 198, 211
dividend   40, 64, 77, 89, 94-95, 106, 194, 209, 210

economy, effect of 34, 163, 168, 176, 180
employees 31, 40-42, 106, 121-122, 168-170, 180, 203
entertainment expense 41-42, 202, 209
estate planning 14, 16
financial projections 29, 81-84
financial ratios 181
financial statement 16, 20, 26, 28, 34-41, 44, 46, 51,
    60- 63, 70-72, 78, 81-83, 89-96, 99-100, 105-108,
    111, 117, 130, 152-155, 167, 176, 181-185, 194,
    196, 199-203, 207-209, 213, 215
    adjusting 6, 16, 26, 35-39, 42-47, 51-56, 60-62,
       66, 70-72, 75, 78, 81-83, 89-101, 105,   107-108,
       130, 150-158, 167-169, 171-178, 181-185, 192, 209,
       213, 214
financing 21, 45, 54, 58, 64, 70, 76, 77, 86, 99,
    104-109, 157, 163, 174-177, 183, 185, 200, 210, 216
goodwill 51, 62, 73, 87, 97, 99, 106, 109, 110, 114,
    115, 119, 123, 125-129, 175, 190, 192, 196, 200,
inflation 34, 59, 63, 69, 74, 86, 102, 106, 111, 126,
    162, 180, 211
insurance 14, 17, 33, 41, 52-53, 77, 100, 155-156,
    162, 191, 195, 202-203, 209
intangible assets 52, 73, 101, 110, 114-116, 120,
    121, 125, 129, 160, 190-192, 203
interest 6, 10, 22-23, 32-39, 43-47, 58-66, 75-80,
    85-86, 89, 93, 96, 104-108, 125, 149-154, 157,
    161-164, 176-182, 195-201, 206, 209-211, 214-216
inventory 29, 45, 61, 73-76, 81-85, 101-104, 107,
    112, 159-161, 168-169, 190-193, 201-205, 217
IRS 16, 38, 40, 62, 72, 80, 110, 120, 128, 176,
lease 29, 32-33, 38, 43, 61, 68, 102, 152, 164,
    192, 203-204, 224
leveraged buyout 50, 52, 67, 77, 87, 106, 124, 204
liabilities 9-10, 19, 28, 45, 50-52, 64, 68, 81,
    84-88, 96-97, 103, 106-109, 114, 122, 124, 129,
    169, 170-174, 193-195, 198, 203, 206-207, 217
LIFO 75, 102, 161, 204-205
liquidation value 51, 75, 87, 97, 110-114, 123,
    125, 158, 160-162, 205-206
loan amount 54, 75, 158, 160, 162
loan security 32, 54, 64, 76, 92, 159-163, 176,
    186, 188, 215-216
loans 20, 32, 43, 50, 54, 57-58, 61-67, 70, 76-78,

80, 85-86, 89, 93, 101, 104, 125, 157-164, 176,
  185-188, 190-193, 195, 197, 199, 204, 209, 214-216
machinery 8, 29, 43, 63, 73-81, 101-107, 112, 115,
  124, 159-162, 191-193, 199, 202, 203, 217
market value 14, 51, 75, 87, 100, 106-113, 125,
  152-158, 164, 172, 178-190, 193, 206, 207
minority stock interest 177
multiples 8, 53, 91, 96, 105, 150-156, 182, 207
negotiation 5, 8, 13, 17-23, 52-57, 104, 113-114,
  123-126, 153-154, 166-167, 172-173, 182, 189,
obsolescence 29, 102-103, 159, 162, 169, 196
P/E ratio 53, 154, 182
patent 116-117, 120-121, 125, 168, 191, 192
perquisites 34, 209, 214
pre-paid expenses 191, 211
preferred stock 64, 77, 89, 194, 209, 210
present value 50, 65, 68, 86-88, 117-122, 130,
  168, 179, 197-199, 211-212, 219
privately-held corp. 17, 44, 52-53, 149-154, 194,
pro forma 35, 70-71, 93, 167, 184-185, 213-214
publicly held corp. 10, 38, 53, 92, 151-155, 170,
  177, 182, 194, 214
purchase of assets 19, 173
purchase of stock 107, 124, 173
real estate 8, 43, 63, 72-76, 81, 92-95, 102-104,
  112, 114, 126, 150, 159, 162-164, 193, 203
replacement value 15, 51, 100, 155, 162
revolving loan 76-86, 89, 160
salaries 31, 34-35, 38-42, 46, 60, 121-122, 178, 199,
  202, 208-209
seller financing 163, 175-176
tax credit 62, 79, 89, 189, 214
tax losses 120, 175
taxes 13, 16, 19, 32, 38-46, 50-53, 57, 60-66, 70-80,
  85, 89, 92-97, 100, 105-108, 114, 117, 119-121,
  127-130, 150, 153-155, 164, 168-169, 173-178, 182,
  189-196, 199, 201-203, 205-206, 208, 210, 214-215
travel expense 41-42, 202, 209
turnaround 67, 111, 216
unsecured loans 64, 77, 89, 176-177, 214-215
weighted average 59, 60, 69-70, 100, 108, 205, 216-217
working capital 61, 64, 76, 81, 85, 93, 103, 104,
  107, 159-161, 217-218

ORDER FORM

Charter Oak Press
Post Office Box 7783
Lancaster, PA 17604-7783

Please send me my <u>own</u> copy of the <u>Business Valuation Manual</u>.

_____ copies at $29.95 each

Pennsylvanians: Please add 6% sales tax.

Shipping: $1 for the first book and .25 for each additional book.

Name:_____

Address:_____

_____ Zip:_____

_____ I can't wait 3-4 weeks for Book Rate delivery. Here is $2.50 per book for Air Mail.